... ; size, 1¼, 1½
...83. Eureka, 1¼
...lock; size, 1¼
.......................15c
...4. Eureka
...x1¼ inches........10c
...2, 8x2 inches
.........................15c

the highest type of perfection in durability, workmanship and material. Nothing better made. Size, which includes shackle, 3⅛ inches, two keys furnished with each lock. Price, each, 60c; per doz...**$7.00**
No. 13894. Same as above lock as above with 10 inch japanned chain. Price, each...**75c;** per doz...**$5.50**

Lever Padlocks.

No. 13896. 6-Lever Padlocks are the finest, safest and most durable padlocks sold at a reasonable price. Cast bronze outside. Brass inside. Phosphor bronze spring guaranteed not to rust or give out under the influence of any climate. Two nickel-plated flat steel keys with each lock. Price, 3½x2¼, weight 6 oz. Price, each...**35c**
No. 13897. Same lock as above, with tinned iron chain attached. Price, each...**35c**

Special patent 6-Lever Padlocks. Made of the same material as our 13896. Has heavy elongated shackle. Just the thing for gate or barn, as the long shackle will permit a chain or heavy staple being used. Complete, with two flat steel keys. No. 13898. Price, each...**40c**
Same lock as above, with 9 inch tinned chain. No. 13899. Price, each...**50c**

No. 13900. Nickel-Plated Brass Padlocks. Just the thing for small boxes, bags or dog collars. Size, 1¼ inch. Price, each, 15c; per doz...**$1.75**
No. 13901. 1½ inch. Price, each, 20c; per doz...**$2.15**
No. 13902. 1¼ inch. Price, each, 22c; per doz...**$2.40**

Secure Lever Locks.

These locks cannot be picked except by a professional, and no key will unlock them unless it is the original key. Each lock has two secure levers. We carry a full line of sizes. Note size carefully when ordering. Keys all different in a dozen.
No. 13925. Secure Lever Chest Lock. Double link, made of iron, size 1½x1¼ inches, key pin ½ inch from top of lock. Price, each, 30c; per doz...**$2.16**
No. 13926. Secure Lever Chest Lock. Double link, made of iron, size 2⅛ inches, key pin ¾ inch from top of lock. Price, each, 34c; per doz...**$3.23**
No. 13927. Secure Lever Chest Lock. Double link, made of iron, size 2½x2¼ inches, key pin ¾ inch from top of lock. Price, each, 40c; per doz...**$4.60**
No. 13928. Secure Lever Chest Lock. Double link, made of iron, size 3x2 inches, key pin ⅞ inch from top of lock. Price, each, 54c; per doz...**$6.24**
No. 13929. Secure Lever Chest Lock. Double link, made of iron, size 3½x2¼ inches, key pin 1 inch from top of lock. Price, each, 80c; per doz...**$8.64**
No. 13930. Secure Lever Chest Lock. Double link, made of iron, size 4x2½ inches, key pin 1¼ inches from top of lock. Price, each, 90c; per doz...**$9.37**

In Gold-Filled and Silver Bracelets we handle nothing but the finest quality, and our line embraces all of the desirable patterns on the market. Chain Bracelets are now the most stylish. They are all full length and are adjustable. Our Gold-Filled Bracelets are all warranted to wear and retain their color for twenty years.

...es' Gold-Filled Bracelet, plain polished links, with raised, ornamented and ... 5 inches. Price, $1.15
...ld Sterling Silver, with satin-finished links, raised, ornamented and satin ...h 5 inches. Price, 95 cents.

...6911. Gold-Filled Bracelet, best quality, bright polished trace pattern links, polished lock. ...75.

...6912. Gold-Filled Bracelet, best quality, fancy chased links, raised, ornamented and polished ... Price, $2.00

...913. Gold-Filled Bracelet, best quality, with fancy chased links, raised, ornamented and ...lock. Price, $2.45
...013. Solid Sterling Silver, chased satined links, raised, ornamented and satin finished lock.

IN ORDERING SINGLE REVOLVERS WE ADVISE SENDING BY MAIL.

This can be done where enough express cent per oz., or fraction thereof. You examination, on receipt of $1.00 as a guarantee of good faith. You can examine the revolver at the express actly as represented, pay the express agent the balance and express charges and the revolver is yours. T companies your order. We advise sending cash in full, deducting 3 per cent. for cash, and adding enough t the revolver sent by mail.

Our 68c Revolver.

No. 876½ "Defender," wood handle, full nickel plated, plain cylinder, 7 shot, .22 caliber, rim fire, safe and reliable. Each...**$0.68**
Postage, extra, 10c.

Our 85c Revolver.

No. 877. Rosewood handle, 7 shot, full nickel plated, .22 caliber, long or short, rim fire, weight, 2, 2½ inch barrel, safe and reliable. Price...**85c**
No. 877½. Rubber Handle, 7 shot, .22 caliber, long or short, rim fire, full nickel plated, weight 7 ounces, rifled barrel. Our special price...**95c**

Defender, 32 Caliber.

No. 878. Rubber Handle, 5 shot, .32 caliber, rim fire, full nickel plated, weight 10 ounces, rifled barrel.
Our special price...**$1.20**
Wood handle—same as above...**$0.85**
For 18c extra we will send by open mail. For 18c extra we will send by registered mail.

Bull Dog Revolvers.

American Bull Dogs are double action, self-cocking. All have rubber stocks, all beautifully nickel plated; all have octagon barrels, all warranted to wear and in perfect order. Regular retail price $5.00; our special price...
Description: These revolvers are strictly first-class in every respect. The quality of material and workmanship is the best. All have rifled barrels and are good shooters; all 5 shot. These are not toys, but good guns. No one can meet our prices on these goods. 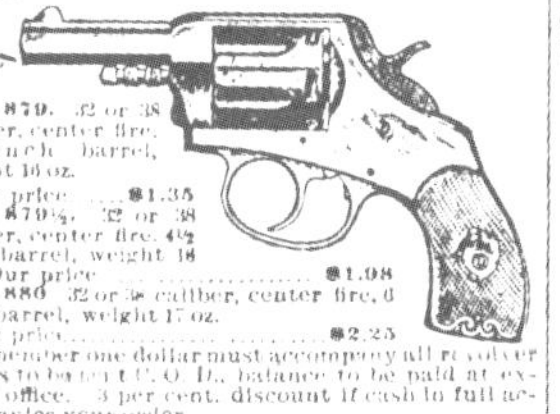
No. 879. .32 or .38 caliber, center fire, 2¼ inch barrel, weight 14 oz.
Our price...**$1.35**
No. 879½. .32 or .38 caliber, center fire, 4½ inch barrel, weight 16 oz.
Our price...**$1.98**
No. 880. .32 or .38 caliber, center fire, 6 inch barrel, weight 17 oz.
Our price...**$2.25**
Remember one dollar must accompany all revolver orders to be sent C. O. D., balance to be paid at express office. 3 per cent. discount if cash in full accompanies your order.
For 20c extra we will send by open mail, postpaid.
For 28c extra we will send by registered mail, postpaid.
No. 880½. Rubber handle, 7 shot, .22 caliber, long or short rim fire, full nickel plated, weight 7 oz., rifled barrel, price...**$1.35**
Postage, extra, 10c.

Our $1.45 Revolver.

FREE TO EXAMINATION DOUBLE ACTION AUTOMATIC POLICE REVOLVER FOR HOUSE and POCKET

No. 881. Forehand & Wadsworth New Double Action, Self-Cocking Revolver, full nickel plated, rubber stock, rifled barrel, safe and reliable, accurate, rebounding locks, parts are interchangeable, .32 caliber, 2½ inch octagon barrel, weight 12 ounces.
Our price...**$1.45**
No. 882. .38 caliber, 2¼ inch octagon barrel, 5 shot, weight about 15 oz. Our price...**$1.45**
Postage, extra, 17c.

Our $1.55 Revolver.

No. 883. Forehand & Wadsworth Safety hammer, double action revolver, full nickel plated, rubber stock, rifled barrel, rebounding lock, 5 shot, octagon barrel, 6 shot, weight 12 ounces.
Our price...**$1.55**
No. 884. .38 caliber, 2¼ inch octagon barrel, 5 shot, weight 15 oz. Our price...**$1.55**
Postage, extra, 17c.

Harrington & Richardson Automatic Revolvers.

Our $2.85 Automatic.

No. 885. This revolver would retail in any first-class gun store at from $5 to $6. It is the celebrated Harrington & Richardson improved automatic, self-extracting, double action, self-cocking, revolver, modeled on the Smith & Wesson pattern, beautifully nickel plated, rubber stock, as accurate and durable as any revolver on the market and equal to the Smith & Wesson in shooting. Weight 18½ oz., 3¼ inch barrel, 6 shot, .32 caliber, center fire.
Our price...**$2.85**
No. 886. 5 shot, .38 caliber, central fire.
Our price...**$2.85**
Postage, extra, 22c.

Our $2.70 Revolver.

No. 887. The Celebrated Forehand & Wadsworth Automatic Revolver for $2.70, a revolver that retails at from $5.00 to $6.00. The very latest improved model, automatic shell extractor, rebounding locks, double action, self-cocking, simple and accurate, interchangeable parts made from drop steel forgings. The frame is cast steel, no malleable iron about it, nickel plated throughout, fancy rubber stock; every revolver is fully warranted; length of barrels 3¼ inches; weight 17 oz., entire length 7⅝ inches. The fact that we sold over 10,000 of these revolvers during the last year is evidence of the general satisfaction they give. .32 caliber, Smith & Wesson center fire cartridges, 6 shot.
Our price...**$2.70**
No. 888. .38 caliber, Smith & Wesson center fire cartridges, 6 shot. Our price...**$2.70**
No. 889. Either .32 or .38 caliber with 5 inch barrel. Our price...**$3.45**
We can furnish these revolvers in blued finish when so desired at 50c. extra.
Postage, 25c extra; 5 inch barrels, 35c extra.

NOTICE: Owing to the heavy advance at the factory, the price of Revolvers, our present prices apply to STOCK ON HAND, and are subject to change without notice. Take advantage of our low prices and order at once.

No. 8314. Center fire, .38 caliber, extra long, 38 grains powder, 148 grains lead, for Ballard rifle No. 2, 50 in box, 32c; per 100, $1.47; weight 2¾ lbs.

38 W.C.F.

No. 8315. Winchester (model of '73), center fire, .38 caliber, 40 grains powder, 180 grains lead, in box, using 1 primer.
Per box, 69c; per 100, $1.38; weight 2¼ lbs. per box.

NEW LIGHTNING MAGAZINE RIFLE

No. 8316. Cartridges, center fire, .38 caliber for Colt's slight Repeating Rifle, 40 grains powder, 180 grains lead.
Per box of 50, 70c; per 100, $1.35; weight 2¼ lbs per box.

LONG COLTS, D.A.

No. 8317. Colt's revolver, .41 caliber, center fire long D A), 50 in a box. Per box, 70c; per 100, $1.28; weight 1½ lbs. per box.

WEBLE

No. 8318. Cartridges, Colt's revolver, .41 caliber, center fire (short DA), 50 in a box. Per box, 60c; per 100, $1.15, weight 1¾ lbs, per box.

44 S&W RUSS

No. 8319. .44 cartridges, center fire, Smith & Wesson, Russian model, 23 grains powder, 246 grains lead. 50 in a box. Per box, 70c; per 100, $1.42; weight 2¼ lbs.

LOADI

No. 8320. Cartridges, center fire, .44 for Colt's lightning repeating, rifle, 40 grains powder, 217 grains lead. Per box of 50, 70c; weight

BALLARD & MARLIN

No. 8328. Cartridges, Ballard, Marlin Winchester rifles, center fire, caliber, 40 powder, lead, weight Per box of 20

100...
No. 8329. Cartridges, for Ballard, Marlin and Winchester single shot, .32-40 caliber, 13 grains of powder, 98 grains lead, weight 1¾ lbs. Per 44c; per 100...

98 55 BALLARD & MARLIN

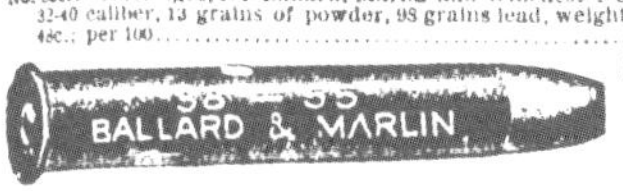

No. 8330. Cartridges, .55 caliber, powder, 2 lead, for Ballard, Marlin, and single shot caliber.
weight, 1¾ lbs.; per 100 $2.72
No. 8331. Cartridges, for Ballard, Marlin and Winchester single shot, .38-short range, 30 grains of powder, 255 grains lead, same length shell. Per box of 20, 60c; per 100...

WINCHESTER MODEL 1886

No. 8332. Cartridges, Winchester rifle, .45-90, Per box of 20, grains, weight, price per 100...

40-60 COLTS NEW LIGHTNING MAGAZINE

No. 8333. Cartridges, center fire, lightning rifle, .50 caliber, 260 grains lead, 1⅓ lbs. Per box; price per 100...

WINCHESTER MODEL 1886

No. 8335. Cartridges, Winchester rifle, .45-70 caliber, 260 grains lead, box of 20, weight 1½ lbs, price per 100...

380 40-60 MARLIN

No. 8336. Cartridges, Marlin rifle, center grains lead, in box. Per box trade price...

No. 8336½. Cartridges for Winchester rifle, model '86, .40-70-330, 20 in bo...

D1710621

... and will give you an ide The Ithaca Gun is so well k to make a full description of In addition to having all of the merless Gun, has the "New A for this gun and is more simp market. That it works direc tained in the lug, makes it lik likely to get out of order. It not only more durable, but ha the other ejectors, which are No. 8286. With fine Engl eered walnut pistol grip stock. Our special price...

THE NEW ITHACA HAMMER GUN FOR $19.95.
This is the late improved model for 1896, manufactured by the Ithaca Gun Co., of Ithaca, New York.

THE CELEBRATED REMIN EJECTOR DOUBLE BA
Grade A. E., automatic ejector; made by the Remington Arms Co., Illion, N. Y. Write for special trade

Law and Order

LIFE IN AMERICA 100 YEARS AGO

Law and Order

James Ciment

Chelsea House Publishers

New York   Philadelphia

CHELSEA HOUSE PUBLISHERS

Editorial Director: Richard Rennert
Executive Managing Editor: Karyn Gullen Browne
Copy Chief: Robin James
Picture Editor: Adrian G. Allen
Creative Director: Robert Mitchell
Art Director: Joan Ferrigno
Production Manager: Sallye Scott

LIFE IN AMERICA 100 YEARS AGO

Senior Editor: Jake Goldberg

Staff for *LAW AND ORDER*
Assistant Editor: Annie McDonnell
Assistant Designer: Lydia Rivera
Picture Researcher: Sandy Jones
Cover Illustrator: Steve Cieslawski

3 5 7 9 8 6 4 2

Library of Congress Cataloging-in-Publication Data

Ciment, James
    Law and Order/James Ciment
    p. cm.—(Life in America 100 years ago)
    Includes bibliographical reference and index.
    Summary: Discusses the law as it has developed in the United States and as it has
pertained to individual liberty, economic growth, social change, and the frontier.
    ISBN 0-7910-2843-7
    1. Law—United States—History—Juvenile literature. [1. Law—History.] I. Title. II. Series.
KE352.Z9C56 1995   94-42471
349.73—dc20   CIP
[347.3]   AC

CONTENTS

LIFE IN AMERICA 100 YEARS AGO

Health and Medicine

Industry

Law and Order

Manners and Customs

Rural Life

Sports and Recreation

Transportation

Urban Life

Law and Order

Law and Individual Liberty

AMERICANS CAN TRACE MANY OF THEIR CHERISHED rights and freedoms back to England. Trial by jury, habeas corpus, and the presumption of innocence were established by precedent and custom, centuries before the Declaration of Independence was proclaimed in 1776.

In May of 1787, however, the founding fathers of the new republic wrote these rights into their Constitution. Several years later, at the insistence of Thomas Jefferson, the Constitutional Convention added a Bill of Rights guaranteeing freedom of speech and assembly, freedom of the press, freedom from unlawful search and seizure, and other rights. The Constitution was a flexible document that could be changed to meet changing times.

But despite their wisdom and foresight, the authors of the Constitution were blinded by the racism of their day. Though it did not mention it by name, the Constitution protected slavery, ensuring a rift between the slaveholding South and the free-labor North. In addition, by leaving the protection of individual rights and other

The signing of the Constitution of the United States of America. As originally conceived, the fundamental law of the land would bring together a people united by common ancestors, language, religion, and customs. But this was hardly the case by 1850. America had become an ethnically diverse nation of 23 million inhabitants, with almost every ethnic group and language in the world represented. Yet the Constitution did not protect the rights of women, black Americans, or Native Americans, and opportunities for recent immigrants were limited if they did not desire to serve as cheap labor.

The whipping post and pillory in New Castle, Delaware, in 1868. Corporal punishment of criminals was an accepted practice before modern times, and the punishment was often administered in public.

important powers to the states, the Constitution left open several questions between the states and the federal government. Who came first? Who was sovereign over whom? Who could dissolve the bonds between them?

These issues were at the center of the long and savage Civil War, fought from 1861 to 1865. After the war, the triumphant North banned slavery with the Thirteenth Amendment in December 1865. Establishing full civil rights for African Americans, however, would prove more difficult.

Charles Sumner, who succeeded Daniel Webster as senator from Massachusetts, was another staunch antislavery advocate. In 1856, in Congress, he gave one of his most famous antislavery speeches, "Crime Against Kansas," protesting the statewide turmoil caused by the Kansas-Nebraska Act. In the speech, Sumner made some inflammatory comments about a South Carolina senator. Though the senator was not present, his cousin, Representative Preston Brooks, was. Brooks beat Sumner severely with a cane in his Senate office. It took Sumner three years to heal from his wounds, after which he was reelected to the Senate. A radical abolitionist, Sumner visited President Lincoln almost every day, pleading for the freedom of African Americans.

Thaddeus Stevens served in the House of Representatives from 1849 to 1853 and again from 1859 to 1868. He was a tough, uncompromising antislavery advocate who also believed in full civil and political equality for blacks.

A wood engraving depicting an escaped slave who joined the Union army. Almost 200,000 blacks fought in the Union army, and more than 38,000 gave their lives for emancipation. Other escaped slaves worked for the North as teamsters, cooks, carpenters, scouts, and day laborers. In one daring and courageous act, two Charleston, South Carolina, slaves, Robert Small and his brother, seized a Confederate sidewheel steamer, the *Planter*, and maneuvered it out of the harbor to the Union fleet.

During the war, 180,000 blacks served gallantly in the Union army. This service, black leaders and their white allies argued, earned black men (women were another matter) full citizenship, including the right to vote. Andrew Johnson, a Democrat who occupied the presidency after the assassination of Abraham Lincoln in April 1865, thought differently. A Tennessean who had remained loyal to the Union, Johnson sympathized with his southern compatriots. In 1865, with Congress out of session, he offered the southern states a blanket pardon in exchange for an end to formal slavery and a signed loyalty oath to the Union.

The South readily accepted these conditions. Soon state legislatures were filled with the old Confederate leaders. In fact, the senator-elect from Georgia, Alexander Stephens, was the former vice-president of

On February 1, 1865, Congress approved the Thirteenth Amendment to the Constitution, abolishing slavery forever. Immediately after the war, the government had taken some honest steps to help newly freed African Americans. Troops were kept in the South, many of them black, and the Bureau of Freedmen, Refugees, and Abandoned Lands was established to help blacks find schooling and jobs at fair wages.

the Confederacy. Across the South, new laws known as Black Codes were passed by state legislatures to ensure the continued subservience, if not outright enslavement, of black Americans. The laws were harsh and discriminatory. For example, each January, African Americans in Mississippi had to get written proof of employment for the coming year or go to jail. Those who left their jobs before their contracts expired could be arrested by any white citizen.

Mississippi blacks were also subject to new vagrancy laws. Anyone who was declared idle, disorderly, or who might "misspend what they earn" could be fined. Other criminal offenses under the Mississippi Black Codes included "insulting" gestures or language,

In 1866, Thomas Nast drew this complex cartoon for *Harper's Weekly* satirizing President Andrew Johnson's "soft" Reconstruction policy toward the South. President Johnson is compared to Shakespeare's villain Iago, who betrayed a black Othello. Northerners were increasingly disturbed by the Ku Klux Klan's terrorism and southern states that established Black Codes to perpetuate discrimination.

"malicious mischief," or preaching the gospel without a license. Naturally, if lawbreakers could not pay their fines, they were sent to jail. Often, the sheriffs or wardens hired out the prisoners to white planters. Once again, many blacks in Mississippi were picking cotton by force and without pay.

Mississippi was not unique. In South Carolina, blacks could not pursue any nonfarming occupation unless they posted an expensive bond. Black domestic employees were required to sign annual contracts that included labor from sunup to sundown. No black could leave a plantation or entertain guests without the written permission of his "master." The old passes of the slave regime had been resurrected.

The African-American family, often brutally separated during the days of slavery, also came under attack from the Black Codes. Throughout the South, legislatures passed "apprenticeship laws" that bound black children to white planters if a judge deemed the parents unable to support them. In North Carolina, fully 10 percent of these

This 1867 illustration from *Harper's Weekly* depicts a black freedman voting for the first time as a result of the Fifteenth Amendment. In that year, more than 700,000 blacks voted. The newly freed black voters were the backbone of the Republican party in the South.

"children" were over 16, including an "orphan" working in a turpentine mill to support his wife and child.

Southern governments intended to bind African Americans to the plantations without actually calling them slaves. And just in case these laws didn't do the trick, other rules were passed that made it virtually impossible for blacks to support themselves economically. Throughout the South, it became illegal for blacks to hunt, fish, gather berries, or own a dog or a gun. All of these laws were enforced by newly formed, all-white militias, many still wearing their Confederate army uniforms.

The newly freed slaves did not take this lying down. With the help of the Freedmen's Bureau, a relief agency founded by Congress in March 1865, freedpersons established their own farms, got an education, and rebuilt families torn apart by slavery and war. Above all else, African Americans wanted the right to own land, which they felt would make true freedom possible. "Forty acres and a mule" became their rallying cry.

They had many allies in the North, particularly among Lincoln's Republican party. Over 300,000 northern men had given their lives in a war started, Republican politicians pointed out, by Democrats and white southerners. Now, it appeared, northern sacrifices had come to naught. Confederate leaders were back in power and slavery had returned in all but name.

This was unacceptable to many Republicans, but so were black demands for land. While a few radical Republicans like Thaddeus Stevens and Charles Sumner advocated seizing the planters' land and giving it to the newly freed slaves, moderate Republicans disagreed. Taking property from one class of Americans and giving it to another, they believed, set a dangerous and unconstitutional precedent.

17

Moreover, with land of their own, African Americans might be unwilling to harvest the cotton crop, a critical American export.

Moderates and radicals did agree, however, that civil rights had to be extended to blacks. In April of 1866, Congress overrode Andrew Johnson's veto and passed the first Civil Rights Bill. It gave blacks the right to own and rent property, to make binding contracts, and to have access to the courts. It also authorized federal authorities to bring suit against anyone who violated these rights. But it made blacks pay for the land seized from planters during the war.

Many congressmen did not feel the Civil Rights Bill was enough. Laws could be overturned by a future Congress, they reasoned, while constitutional amendments could not. In April of 1866, the Joint Committee on Reconstruction submitted a draft for the Fourteenth Amendment, easily the most complicated amendment in the Constitution and perhaps the most important.

The amendment had five sections. The first two concerned black citizenship. It guaranteed that all persons born or naturalized in the United States were citizens, and that no state could deny them their rights. If any state was to deny a male citizen the right to vote, it would lose a proportion of its representation in Congress. For the first time, the federal government guaranteed every American's citizenship rights.

Sections three and four covered the recent insurrection. Any representative of the Confederate government, any officer in the Confederate military, or anyone who had aided the Confederacy in any substantial way could not run for elected office. All former Confederates elected under Johnson's amnesty would be stripped of office. Finally, section five gave Congress the power to enforce the provisions of the amendment.

An 1868 drawing of two Ku Klux Klan members. In their attempt to topple Republican control, southern whites resorted to harassment and brutality. Secret societies like the Klan were basically terrorist organizations that tried to prevent blacks from voting. In spite of their intimidation, African Americans continued to vote in substantial numbers. But violence against blacks escalated, and by the 1890s an average of 187 lynchings took place annually.

President Johnson, of course, vehemently opposed the amendment and successfully urged enough southern states to vote it down, denying the amendment the three-quarters majority required to make it part of the Constitution. This action inflamed a northern public tired of concessions to the South. Race riots in Memphis and in New Orleans, where white mobs murdered 37 blacks at a suffrage convention, reenforced the antisouthern sentiments of northern voters. In the congressional elections of 1866, Republicans gained sweeping majorities in both houses of Congress and every northern state legislature. In March, Congress overrode another Johnson veto

19

This 1870 woodcut shows a courtroom with a jury composed of both blacks and whites.

and passed the Reconstruction Act of 1867, a radical measure that placed the states of the former Confederacy under military rule. In order to return to the Union, voters had to accept new state constitutions guaranteeing black suffrage, and they had to ratify the Fourteenth Amendment.

During 1868, six southern states—Alabama, Arkansas, Florida, Louisiana, and the Carolinas—met the requirements, putting the Fourteenth Amendment into the Constitution. In February of 1869, Congress passed the Fifteenth Amendment, forbidding states from denying citizens the right to vote on the basis of race, color, or "previous condition of servitude." Radicals wanted the amendment to be broader and include bans on property requirements and literacy tests. But many northern states, such as California with its large Chinese population, wanted to use these methods to deny Asian immigrants the right to vote.

The Fourteenth and Fifteenth amendments brought a new order to the South. Republicans took control of every southern state, remaining in power from a few months in Virginia to over nine years in South Carolina, Louisiana, and Florida. Between 1866 and 1876, sixteen blacks were elected to the Senate and the House of Representatives, including Mississippi's Hiram Revels, elected to fill former Confederate president Jefferson Davis's pre–Civil War seat in the Senate.

At the state level, many blacks served in state legislatures. Louisiana had a black governor and a black lieutenant governor, while Mississippi and South Carolina both had black lieutenant governors. At the local level, blacks served as sheriffs and judges and formed militia companies to protect their newly won citizenship rights. But they rarely ruled alone. While blacks formed a majority in the lower house of the South Carolina legislature, elsewhere they formed alliances with white politicians, including many who had moved from the North after the war to promote their liberal and progressive agendas in other states.

Before the Civil War, the South had lagged behind the North socially and economically. It had few publicly supported institutions like hospitals, asylums, and schools. And it lacked an industrial base. In addition, many southern states still had laws on the books that permitted imprisonment for debt and banned divorce. Reconstruction governments set out to modernize their states with new laws, new institutions, and new bonds to pay for railroads and industry.

21

To raise funds, they passed new taxes, often on land held by disenfranchised planters.

With all this money passing through government hands, corruption flourished. South Carolina businessman "Honest John" Patterson bribed the legislature with $45,000 to obtain his seat in the U.S. Senate (until the Seventeenth Amendment in 1913, state legislatures elected senators). Georgia businessman John Bryant received $30,000 from the Harper Brothers publishing house after he got the education superintendent to adopt their textbooks for the state school system.

Many white southerners resented the new taxes and the corruption. Ignorant black politicians and government officials, they said, were being manipulated by northern businessmen known as "carpetbaggers" and southern opportunists called "scalawags."

But to white southerners, the most galling aspect of the new regime was something more basic: black power. To a white population raised on the idea of blacks as slaves—"a mudsill class," a pre–Civil War South Carolina senator had called them—there was strong resistance to living with blacks as equals. The sight of black sheriffs on the streets and the presence of black judges in the courts threatened the centuries-old system of white supremacy. New laws imposing $1,000 fines on civil rights violators in South Carolina, Louisiana, and Florida made many white southerners feel they had lost control of their governments.

Locked out of power by black-white liberal majorities—and sometimes disenfranchised under the Fourteenth Amendment—white southerners turned to extralegal methods to reassert their control over southern society. Some turned to terrorism. By 1870, the Ku Klux Klan was operating throughout the South as a secret army serving the opposition Democratic party. The Klan murdered Republican politicians, burned black schools and churches, and attacked black political rallies. Blacks defended themselves but were often outgunned. The struggle reached a climax when Klansmen laid siege to Colfax, Louisiana, in 1873. For three weeks, black veterans defended the town until Klansmen brought in cannons. On Easter Sunday, 50 blacks and 2 whites were slaughtered when they tried to surrender under a white flag.

The federal government responded with anti-Klan acts in 1870 and 1871, making it a federal offense to deprive citizens of the right to vote, hold office, serve on juries, and enjoy equal protection under the law. This was the first time the government had made private criminal acts violations of federal law, an action made possible by the Fourteenth Amendment. Another Civil Rights Act in 1875 attempted to end discrimination in hotels, theaters, and railroads, though not in schools.

It was not enough. The Klan had widespread support throughout the South, making criminal prosecution difficult in the absence of what one southern Republican called "a steady, unswerving power from without." And, indeed, northern concern was wavering. With the world economy descending after 1873 into history's first great industrial depression, northern voters turned their attention from civil rights to economic survival.

This combination of northern indifference and Klan terrorism brought down Reconstruction governments one by one throughout the South. Finally, in 1877, to settle a contentious presidential election in their favor, the Republicans agreed to pull the last federal troops out of the South, dooming the remaining Reconstruction regimes in Florida, Louisiana, and South Carolina. With all-white regimes back

23

In 1892, Homer Adolph Plessy, an African American, boarded a train in New Orleans and dared to sit in the white section. He was ordered to leave the car, and when he refused he was arrested. While he admitted to violating the state law, he claimed that the state had no right to make such a law according to the Constitution. The lower court judge who ruled against Plessy was named Ferguson. The case reached the Supreme Court, and in the famous *Plessy v. Ferguson* decision, the Court decided that "separate but equal" public facilities did not violate the Constitution. This decision was a major blow against the hard-won rights of African Americans, and the separate but equal doctrine dominated American law for the next 70 years.

in power, black sheriffs, militia, and judges disappeared. And with
them, blacks lost the protection they had once had against dishonest
merchants and dictatorial planters. They were again forced to sign
unfair sharecropping contracts, placing themselves in permanent
debt to their landlords.

"Redemption," the religious term white southerners used to
describe the return of white supremacy, was now complete. The
experiment in black and white power sharing and the federal
protection of civil rights ceased for another 70 years.

The unraveling of civil rights protection began in 1873 with the
Louisiana "Slaughterhouse" cases, in which the Supreme Court
declared that the federal government was responsible for federal
rights only. Thus, if whites prevented blacks from voting in state
elections, the state was responsible. Then, in October 1883, the
Supreme Court declared the Civil Rights Act of 1875 unconstitutional.
The majority opinion argued that blacks must cease "to be the special
favorite of the laws."

Still, many blacks retained the right to vote under Redemption
governments, though this vote was often manipulated and controlled
by local planters and merchants. In the 1880s, however, a political
movement called populism swept through the South. Appealing to
poor whites and blacks to lay aside their racial differences for a
common cause, populism threatened the political and economic
control of planters and merchants.

The planters and merchants responded to the populists by
playing up fears of "Negro domination." The effort was successful.
The planters maintained their power by offering poor whites a
privileged middle place in society, economically poor but politically
and socially superior to blacks. Soon states throughout the South

25

A lithograph depicting the first African-American senators and representatives elected to Congress. Between 1869 and 1901, 20 black Americans were elected to the House and 2 were elected to the Senate.

were disenfranchising black voters with poll taxes, literacy tests, and property requirements—methods that also took away the right to vote from some of the poorest whites. In 1898, Louisiana came up with a way to ensure that only blacks would lose the vote. A "grandfather clause" was added to the literacy and property tests that exempted those entitled to vote on January 1, 1867—before blacks got suffrage—along with their sons and grandsons.

While the Supreme Court, under the prodding of the newly formed National Association for the Advancement of Colored People (NAACP), declared "grandfather clauses" unconstitutional in 1915, it affirmed other disenfranchising methods in its 1898 *Williams v. Mississippi* decision. The effect on black voter participation was devastating. Louisiana, for example, had 164,088 registered white voters and 130,344 black voters in 1896. After the "grandfather clause" in 1900, 125,437 whites registered to vote, but the number of black voters declined to 5,320. In 1901, the last black congressman of the 19th century, North Carolina's George White, lost his seat.

Disenfranchisement was only one part of the legal assault on black rights in the late 19th century. Planters fueled white fears of social integration in an effort to counter poor white–black political alliances. Southern governments enacted segregation, or "Jim Crow" laws, to prevent a recurrence of the populist threat. Beginning with Florida in 1887, blacks and whites were legally separated in hotels, restaurants, trains, and other public places throughout the South.

Blacks challenged "Jim Crow" as a violation of the Fourteenth Amendment, which guaranteed equal treatment under the law for all U.S. citizens. But in its infamous 1896 *Plessy v. Ferguson* decision, the Supreme Court ruled that a Louisiana segregation statute was constitutional as long as it assured that the accommodations for blacks and whites were "separate but equal." It was, as one historian called it, "an act of willful blindness" on the part of the Supreme Court. Segregated facilities were rarely if ever equal, and segregation was designed to underscore the inferiority of blacks.

Law and Economic Growth

ALONG WITH A BLUEPRINT FOR GOVERNMENT AND AN outline for civil rights, the Constitution laid the legal groundwork for the nation's economy. More specifically, the Constitution defined the all-important relationship between business and government.

   Responding to the weak Articles of Confederation, the Constitution's authors made sure the new document would promote economic growth. They did this in two ways. First, they made all internal customs and duties unconstitutional. Merchants would be free to trade in any of the states without fear of prejudicial legislation favoring local businessmen. In addition, the Constitution placed the regulation of all interstate commerce under the control of Congress. Second, they made it unconstitutional for any state to pass ex post facto laws, guaranteeing that contracts could not be canceled by the acts of state governments. In addition, they placed the power to write bankruptcy laws with Congress. In short, the Constitution would protect the sanctity of contracts.

29

A cartoon from the 1880s depicting America as Prometheus bound to the rock by predatory monopolists. Congressmen on the payroll of monopolists are shown as the snake. In the lower left is the crawling snail of legislative action, with a sleeping person on top symbolizing the people's rights. Monopolies were causing unstable economic conditions, with painful recessions occurring every five or six years after 1873.

The Constitution's economic provisions bore fruit. Between its final ratification in 1789 and the outbreak of the Civil War in 1861, the American economy grew steadily. By the latter date, America's industrial output—centered mostly in the Northeast and the upper Midwest—was second only to Great Britain's.

During the first half of the 19th century, state and federal governments saw it as their duty to unleash economic activity. Government investment in turnpikes and canals helped overcome the problem of transportation across an expansive country. And tariffs, or

The worst depression of the 19th century occurred in 1873, when Jay Cooke and Company, a leading investment banking firm, overextended its investments in postwar railroad construction and failed. The depression lasted six years. An easy credit policy would have eased the situation, but President Grant wanted debtors to pay what they owed in "sound" currency based on gold reserves. Debtor groups, like farmers, wanted the Treasury to issue more greenbacks, the paper currency first printed in 1862 to help fund the Union war effort. The Greenback party emerged in 1876 to champion this cause.

taxes on imports, protected infant industries from destructive foreign competition.

Equally important were several court decisions concerning tort and corporate law. Tort law covers noncriminal injuries or wrongs done by one private citizen to another. An insignificant branch of law before 1800, tort law grew in importance with the rise of property damage and personal injuries caused by the machines of the industrial revolution, especially railroads.

In a series of English legal decisions in the 1830s and 1840s—decisions adopted by American judges—the courts ruled that businesses were not absolutely liable for the damages they caused. This was an important piece of legal reasoning. If a railroad company was liable for every fire started by a spark from its locomotives, it would be

31

While the industrial revolution produced enormous economic growth, it also created many problems, such as child labor. The National Child Labor Committee, formed in 1905, tried to mount a public protest that would force through Congress legislation abolishing child labor. The committee's freelance investigator and photographer, Lewis Hine, became famous for his poignant, arresting photographs of working children. His first story was about messengers, newsboys, and vendors under 12 years of age working night hours from 8 P.M. to 4 A.M. During the 12 years he worked as the committee's investigator, Hine covered many work sites and used clever disguises to gain entrance.

This 1889 cartoon on the front page of *Puck* shows monopolists and their allies busily manipulating the legal system for their own advantage.

The Homestead Riot of 1892. The Homestead plant near Pittsburgh was a major steel mill owned by the Carnegie Steel Company. Here the Amalgamated Association of Iron and Steel Workers was a powerful force. Andrew Carnegie wanted the union out, and he plotted to undermine its power. When the union refused to accept a decrease in wages and called a strike, Carnegie hired 300 Pinkerton guards to protect the nonunion workers he planned to hire as replacements. The workers met the Pinkerton guards with guns and dynamite. Three guards and 10 strikers were killed and many more were injured. Public opinion was initially on the side of the workers, until a Polish-born radical, Alexander Berkman, tried unsuccessfully to assassinate one of Carnegie's managers. The governor of Pennsylvania then sent 8,000 National Guardsmen to protect the strikebreakers. The union was broken and workers returned to their jobs four months later.

bankrupted. The judges ruled that the railroads would not be responsible for damages if they took reasonable precautions in the conduct of their business.

This trend in tort law was further developed in the 1840s and 1850s by the development of the concept of "contributory negligence." In its 1852 *Haring v. New York and Erie Railroad Company* decision, the New York State Supreme Court said that the railroad was not liable for injuries when its locomotive struck a wagon at a crossing since the wagon's driver, who was not looking, was partially responsible for the accident.

The "fellow servant" rule applied this reasoning to a company's employees. In 1842, the Massachusetts Supreme Court ruled that

because one worker on the Boston and Worcester Railroad was partially responsible for the injury to another—typical of industrial accidents—the company was not liable. The worker could, of course, sue his fellow worker. But since that worker was likely to be as poor as the injured plaintiff, the suit would be worthless.

During these same years, state legislatures and courts made it easier for a new form of business—the corporation—to operate. The corporate form allowed a number of investors to pool their financial resources and appoint people to manage its affairs. The investors would only be liable for the amount they invested. This limited liability seemed suspicious, and so in the beginning incorporation was usually reserved for nonprofit groups such as charities and municipalities.

Beginning in the early 19th century, corporations began to be formed for profitable purposes. To form a corporation, the investors had to get a special charter from the state legislature. This charter specified exactly what the corporation could do, and it often granted the investors a monopoly to do it. However, chartered monopolies could also dampen economic growth.

For that reason, the idea of monopoly privilege was overturned by two important Supreme Court decisions: *Gibbons v. Ogden* in 1824 and *Charles River Bridge v. Warren Bridge* in 1837. In the latter case, the Charles River Bridge Company had been granted a monopoly charter by the Massachusetts legislature to build a bridge over the Charles River. Chief Justice Roger Taney overthrew the charter. "While the rights of private property are sacredly guarded," he ruled, "we must not forget that the community also has rights, and the happiness and well-being of every citizen depends on their faithful preservations." Competition, he explained, was important to economic growth and economic growth was good for the people.

Taney's ruling against monopolized charters was indirectly echoed by the state legislatures. Beginning in the 1840s, states began replacing the special charters with general laws for incorporation, making it cheap and routine to form a corporation. These legal changes—along with population growth, new technology, westward expansion, foreign investment, and government contracts during the Civil War—led to a rapid growth in the number and size of corporations between 1850 and the beginning of the first worldwide industrial depression in 1873.

The sitting room in the New Labor Employment Bureau established by the Commissioners of Charities and Corrections in New York in 1870.

The New York Foundling Asylum, an early orphanage, photographed in 1888.

This was especially true of railroads. By 1873, railroads had become the biggest privately operated institutions in world history. They controlled tens of millions of dollars in capital and equipment, employed thousands of men and women, did most of the nation's long-distance business of hauling goods and passengers, and laid over 60,000 miles of track from coast to coast.

The railroads and other corporations used their immense wealth in dangerous ways. Their directors issued watered stock—that is, shares in excess of the real value of the business—deceiving gullible investors. They forced towns along proposed lines to pay bribes to the corporation or see the tracks laid elsewhere. They received millions of acres in free land from the federal government, often by paying bribes. Corrupt judges issued injunctions against striking workers for a price and, on several occasions, they got the president of the United States to dispatch troops when industrial workers refused to go back to work.

Railroads and other corporations were once seen as necessary for economic growth and the good of the community, but now they were depicted as monsters devouring free enterprise and democratic government. "The offices of our great corporations were secret chambers in which trustees [management] plotted the spoilation of their [communities]," wrote Charles Francis Adams, the son and grandson of U.S. presidents, in 1866. Modern society, he added, had "created a class of artificial beings [corporations] establishing despotisms which no spasmodic popular effort will be able to shake off."

Not that the people didn't try. In the early 1870s, a farmers' movement sprang up in the Midwest called the Grange. Beginning as an educational and social organization, the Grange soon changed its

Dorothea Dix was an extraordinary woman who was instrumental in bringing about several important social reforms. Dix taught a Sunday school class for women in a Massachusetts prison. Appalled by the treatment of the prisoners, particularly of the mentally ill inmates, she traveled throughout the state inspecting prisons and became the first person ever to issue a report on prison conditions. Her investigation of "insane asylums" in other states prompted the opening of new, improved mental institutions and hospitals.

focus to politics, and its main targets were the railroads. Western farmers were angry at the high rates railroads charged to ship their crops. They also did not like the discriminatory rates that made short-haul shippers—such as farmers trying to get their crops to the nearest grain elevators—pay more than long haulers.

In the 1870s, farmers got several state legislatures to pass laws regulating rates charged by railroads and grain elevators. In its 1877 *Munn v. Illinois* decision, the Supreme Court ruled in favor of the Grange, saying that these enterprises involved the public interest and were subject to the police powers of the states. But this was a rare exception to the rule. For the most part, the Supreme Court overturned state laws that tried to regulate corporate behavior. Sometimes, the Court cited the interstate commerce clause of the Constitution. An Indiana statute requiring the prompt delivery of telegraph messages was overturned in 1887 because, the Court ruled, only Congress had the authority to regulate "telegraphic communication between citizens of different states."

Even in the case of intrastate business, the Court found a way to overturn state laws it found hostile to corporate activity. Ironically, they turned to the Fourteenth Amendment, a constitutional measure intended for the newly freed slave. As mentioned earlier, the Fourteenth Amendment guaranteed the protection of equal rights and due process of law to all citizens of the United States. The transition from protecting black citizens to protecting corporate citizens with the Fourteenth Amendment was a circuitous one. It began with the infamous *Slaughterhouse* rulings of 1873. The rulings concerned an 1869 Louisiana statute that limited the butchering of all cattle in New Orleans to one company. This was done for obvious reasons of health and sanitation. But other butchers sued, saying that their right to engage in the work of their choice was protected by the Fourteenth Amendment. The Court ruled against them, arguing that only constitutionally mandated federal rights were protected under the Fourteenth Amendment, and the right to work was not one of them.

While citizens' rights under the Fourteenth Amendment were being circumscribed, corporate rights were being extended beginning with an 1887 decision declaring the Santa Clara Railroad a citizen, with all the same rights and immunities. In 1890, the court used that new definition of corporate citizenship to overturn a Minnesota regulation on the prices the Chicago, Milwaukee, and St. Paul

Railway Company could charge for shipping milk. By not taking the company to court and proving its rates unreasonable, the state had violated the railroad's right to due process under law.

This and other decisions aggravated fears of growing corporate power. Congress responded with the Interstate Commerce Commission (ICC), a federal agency charged with making sure all railroad rates were "reasonable and just." But the commission never had much power to enforce its decisions and what little power it had was stripped away by several Supreme Court decisions in the late 1890s. In an 1897 decision, for instance, the Court ruled that a railroad could charge whatever rates were needed to remain competitive. In other words, there was almost nothing the ICC could do to protect the public against rate hikes.

As many critics of the Supreme Court—including some of its own dissenting members—noted, the majority of justices held to an old-fashioned constitutionalism. They feared the power of the state and underestimated the power of the new corporations. In doing so, they severely hampered the only institution—the federal government—capable of restraining that corporate power and directing it toward the public good.

That outdated outlook was even more devastating to the rights of workers. Rapid industrialization meant that more people were doing unskilled work for wages. But because increased competition meant lower profits, wages were often cut and work stepped up. Often, the only way workers could protest these actions was by striking.

In the early part of the century, these union-organized efforts were prosecuted as conspiracies. But an important Massachusetts ruling in 1842 put this form of prosecution on the road to extinction. Corporations and the judges who supported them then had to find

The Interstate Commerce Act of 1887, grudgingly passed in response to the demands of western farmers for fair practices in setting railroad freight rates, established an independent regulatory commission, the first of its kind, to regulate transportation fees. Here, as Uncle Sam looks on, a group of westerners try to lasso the obstreperous railroad companies.

another way to stop strikes. They discovered it in the injunction, an ancient legal device that could be put to many uses. An injunction could order that a person or group of persons desist in any activities the judge declared were causing someone irreparable damage (such as the loss of profits). In the case of a strike, a judge could use an injunction to stop workers from picketing and allow strikebreakers to enter a factory. In 1894, the courts used this to jail leaders of a strike against the Pullman Sleeping Car Company.

The courts' assaults on workers were not limited to strikes. They also attacked state regulations that limited hours of employment, an important working class issue in an era of 12-hour workdays. Once again, the Supreme Court used old-fashioned reasoning to favor corporate interests. Limiting the hours of employment, they said, denied two free and legally equal citizens—employee and

41

The "Parade of Trusts" trample the people. When Congress passed the Sherman Antitrust Act in 1890, more than a dozen states had already initiated some form of antitrust legislation. The Sherman Antitrust Act was not vigorously enforced until 1901, when Theodore Roosevelt became president.

employer—the right to negotiate any kind of work contract they pleased. This, of course, ignored the fact that a multimillion-dollar corporation and a starving worker were hardly in equal negotiating positions. In 1905, the Supreme Court threw out New York's law limiting the notoriously long hours of city bakers.

Around the turn of the century, however, the tide began to shift. A wave of massive corporate consolidation between 1897 and

1901—culminating in the formation of U.S. Steel, the first billion-dollar corporation—alarmed the public. From 1900 to 1917, during what historians call the Progressive Era, the federal government, including the Supreme Court, made earnest efforts to curb the powers of the corporation. Initially, the Supreme Court began to accept the idea of regulating hours of employment for women and children. In *Muller v. Oregon* (1908), the court ruled that "the future well-being of the race" depended on women and that meant that they should be "protected from the greed . . . of man."

A group of journalists—known as "muckrakers"—exposed the nasty doings of corporations. In his 1906 best-seller *The Jungle,* Upton Sinclair revealed the dangerous and unsanitary working conditions in corporate meat-packing plants in Chicago. As a socialist, Sinclair wanted to help the workers. But the public was more shocked at the idea of eating unhealthy meat. A nationwide system of food production had made it impossible for consumers to really know what went into the food they were eating. The federal government responded with the Food and Drug Administration (FDA), an agency responsible for inspecting and regulating the content of the nation's foods and drugs.

The very bigness of corporations also came under assault, but it took some time to bring down the mighty giants called trusts. The trust was an old legal device put to new corporate use in the late 19th century. It allowed a single board of directors—called trustees—to run many companies in a single industry. Beginning in the 1880s, trusts were formed in the sugar, whiskey, and tobacco industries, among others.

Congress responded to this monopolistic threat to competition with the Sherman Antitrust Act in 1890. Though the act prohibited

George Pullman headed the Pullman Palace Car Company, which manufactured sleeping and parlor cars for the railroads. It was located in a 600-acre company town near Chicago, where the workers rented housing from the company. In 1894, Pullman decided to reduce wages by 25 percent without any decrease in the rents his workers paid him. Eugene Debs, who headed the American Railway Union, organized workers in 27 states not to handle Pullman cars. Governor John Altgeld of Illinois sympathized with the strikers and refused to send in the state militia, but President Grover Cleveland superceded him and sent 2,000 federal troops to the Chicago area. Debs and other union organizers were jailed after a trial without a jury as strikebreakers, protected by soldiers, entered the Pullman plant.

combinations or conspiracy in "restraint of trade," it did not accomplish much. A government effort to break up the sugar trust in Louisiana was thwarted by the Supreme Court in its 1895 *United States v. E.C. Knight Company* decision. According to the Court, the company was in the business of manufacturing, not trade. Therefore the act did not apply. The Court's narrow ruling ignored the fact that the company dictated prices and territories to its distributors.

On the other hand, the Court used a broader interpretation of the act against unions. In the *Danbury Hatters* case of 1908, the Court ruled that a union-organized boycott was a conspiracy in restraint of trade and it fined the union triple damages, threatening the savings and homes of union members.

But several factors combined to put some teeth into corporate regulation. In 1903, Congress reenforced the ICC by giving it the power to ban the rebates railroads offered to preferred customers, that is, other large corporations. In 1906, Congress took another step and passed the Hepburn Act, which allowed the ICC to set maximum rates and inspect railroad company books.

Finally, even antitrust legislation began to be enforced. In 1904, the Supreme Court reversed its *Knight* decision and ordered that the Northern Securities Company, a combination of railroads in the Northwest, be broken up. Still, most government leaders, including the so-called "trust buster" president, Theodore Roosevelt, were wary of breaking up large corporations. Roosevelt, like many others, believed bigness was necessary for modern industry. While "bad trusts" should be broken up, he declared, "good trusts" should be left intact.

One such bad trust was Standard Oil. Founded by John D. Rockefeller in the 1860s, Standard Oil had used unethical, illegal, and monopolistic methods to gain control of nearly 90 percent of the nation's oil business by 1900. An exposé by muckraker Ida Tarbell fired up the public and got the federal government into action. It took years of litigation, but in 1911, Standard Oil was broken up into seven regional oil companies.

In 1914, Congress passed and President Woodrow Wilson signed the Clayton Antitrust Act. The act set up the Federal Trade Commission (FTC), an agency empowered to stop corporate practices "where the effect may be to substantially lessen competition or tend to create a monopoly in any line of commerce." Weak at first, the commission eventually received broad powers to investigate companies and issue "cease and desist" orders against unfair practices that violated antitrust law.

Law and the Lawyer

LAWYERS HAVE NEVER BEEN LOVED IN AMERICAN HISTORY, but they have been indispensable. Jokes about lawyers have circulated since before the Revolution, but the Declaration of Independence and the Constitution were crafted by them.

Maybe lawyers have been so disliked because they are so much a reflection of us. Americans are legalistic and jealous of their rights and freedoms. We need lawyers. At the same time, Americans are materialistic and ambitious, and so are our lawyers. The history of the legal profession is a microcosm of the history of America.

In the pre–Civil War years, a wide-open America possessed a wide-open legal profession. Anyone could be a lawyer. It did not require a long formal education or a battery of examinations. Despite this openness of opportunity, the sons of professionals predominated over the sons of farmers and laborers. In New England—an especially well-educated part of the country in the early 1800s—over 70 percent of practicing lawyers had some college education at a time when a college education was not as common as it is today.

47

The Supreme Court of the United States in 1888. With westward expansion, the growth of industry and monopoly, and the struggles of union workers and the immigrant poor, the Court found itself confronting many new constitutional issues at the turn of the century.

Still, the requirements to practice law in most states were minimal before the Civil War. A legal education, for example, was usually received informally, often by working as an apprentice to a practicing lawyer. Like any apprentice, the student or his parents paid a fee to the lawyer and, in return, the lawyer let him do simple chores like copying documents and sweeping out the office. If the apprentice was fortunate, the lawyer might show him a few tricks of the trade and lend him his notated copies of William Blackstone's *Commentaries,* the indispensable guide to English common law.

Practicing law and teaching law were, of course, two different things. Some lawyers were gifted teachers and gave up practicing to open small law schools. The first law office–law school was founded by Tapping Reeve, a judge in Litchfield, Connecticut, in 1784. Until its demise in 1833, the Litchfield School trained over a thousand students in a 14-month course of lectures and examinations.

Teaching positions, or chairs, were established at a number of universities in the early 1800s, but the first university-affiliated law school opened at Harvard in 1816. While Harvard trained thousands of lawyers before the Civil War and included Supreme Court justice Joseph Story on its faculty, its prestige did not reverse the general lowering of requirements to practice law.

Throughout the early 19th century, it was becoming easier and easier in most states to be admitted to the bar. While some states like New York required a rigorous seven years of preparation, most dropped these requirements. In 1800, 14 out of 19 states or organized territories prescribed a specific time period of preparation. By 1840, only 11 out of 30 states and territories did so.

Examinations were often nothing more than a formality. Salmon Chase, the chief justice of the U.S. Supreme Court from 1864 to 1873, recalled his 1829 Maryland examination. The judge who administered the half-hour examination wanted him to study another year. But when Chase told him he had already "made all . . . the

The first law school in the United States at Litchfield, Connecticut, founded by Judge Tapping Reeve in 1784. There were few law books available in the American colonies, and lessons were based mainly on lectures. The emphasis was on commercial rather than criminal law. Experience and advanced training were obtained through an apprenticeship, that is, by working as a clerk for another practicing lawyer.

arrangements to go to the western country and practice law," the judge swore him in anyway.

Not surprisingly, the practice of law was as informal as the requirements. Unlike England, American states did not develop graded bars where only special lawyers—called solicitors—could practice in front of higher courts. In the United States, virtually any attorney could practice in any court. And passing the bar in one state usually allowed a lawyer to practice in other states.

Competition among lawyers was no more and no less rigorous than in any other business. That is to say, it was fierce indeed. There were no prohibitions on advertising, and lawyers advertised in newspapers and even on courthouse walls. Word of mouth was the most likely way to get business, however, and word of mouth came from reputation. Winning cases was important, but so was style. Legal tricks, courtroom antics, and emotional acting caught the public's attention and helped make a lawyer's reputation. Describing New Hampshire Senator Daniel Webster's courtroom dramatics, an observer noted how "his lips quivered; his firm cheeks trembled with emotion; his eyes were filled with tears, his voice choked . . . he seemed struggling to . . . gain . . . mastery over himself."

A good dramatic style was nothing, however, without a mastery of the spoken word. Courtroom dockets in the pre–Civil War years were less crowded and the pace of trials less hectic than they would be in years to come. There was time for long flights of oratory. Alexander Hamilton, former secretary of the treasury, spoke for six hours in a New York Supreme Court libel suit. "Counsel," an observer of the U.S. Supreme Court noted, "are heard in silence for hours, without being stopped or interrupted."

(continued on page 55)

In this humorous 1889 lithograph, a policeman on a bicycle stops a high-spirited couple on a tandem bicycle for exceeding the speed limit. In the preindustrial era, this was the extent of a police officer's mobility.

A trial scene in a Colorado mining town. As raucous and undisciplined as such trials could be, the people of the frontier very much desired that the rule of law would come to their communities. Only in mythology was the frontier settled by gunslingers, buffalo hunters, and adventurers. It was really settled by immigrant farmers and ranchers who desired tranquillity and economic stability.

53

A scene from the Haymarket Massacre of May 4, 1886, in Chicago, showing police firing into a mob of rioters attacking a patrol wagon. The riot resulted when workers striking the McCormick Harvester Company for an eight-hour workday assembled in Haymarket Square and were fired upon by the police after a bomb was thrown into police ranks.

(continued from page 50)

In the common law tradition, which the United States adopted from England, the written word is even more important than the spoken word. Common law—as opposed to formally enacted legislation, that is, written statutory law—represents the accumulation of reported cases. If a case was not reported, it could not become part of the law. Lawyers need case law like carpenters need wood; they build their cases out of it.

In the 18th century, naturally enough, Americans borrowed their reported case law from England. In 1789, Ephraim Kirby published the first volume of case law entitled *Connecticut Reports.* Alexander Dallas followed the next year with reports on Pennsylvania case law and, in his second volume, cases heard by the Supreme Court, which was located in Philadelphia at the time. By 1830, virtually every state had published reports, though some provided little more than brief abstracts of the decisions.

Practical literature—such as Zephaniah Swift's *System of the Laws of Connecticut*—also began to be published. Soon books on other states' legal systems and general books on evidence, criminal law, and corporate law followed. Most of these avoided legal theory and instead offered practical tips and shortcuts through intricate bodies of legal precedent. The same was true of legal periodicals like *The American Jurist and Law Magazine,* one of five such periodicals in 1830, which offered case notes and question-and-answer materials.

The years following the Civil War brought profound changes in the nation and the legal profession. Rapid urbanization and population growth made for an increasingly complicated nation, while rapid industrialization and corporate growth meant an increasingly complicated economy. The quantity and types of crime, tort, contract, and other realms of law grew exponentially. Courts became busier,

The English jurist Sir William Blackstone, who in the middle of the 18th century helped to codify and popularize English common law. Blackstone's *Commentaries on the Law of England* was a best-seller among lawyers in England and America and was frequently referred to in establishing American legal principles.

A criminal court in New York City in 1853. There was nothing organized about criminal justice in the middle of the 19th century. Detectives, probation officers, public defenders, and forensic scientists did not exist, and for the most part district attorneys worked at other jobs. Petty criminals were usually rushed through the system and sentenced quickly; juries were selected only for serious crimes and they tended to convict; and the only way to be released early was to appeal to the governor for a pardon.

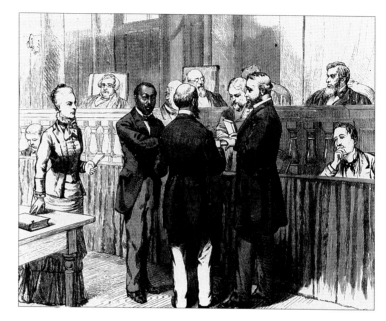

In 1880, the U.S. Supreme Court allowed a black attorney for the first time to argue cases before the Court.

dockets more crowded, and the law more complex. Every aspect of the legal profession had to adjust, beginning with education.

The reforms began, appropriately enough, at the nation's oldest continuously operating law school, Harvard, and were instituted by a man named Christopher Columbus Langdell. Appointed dean in 1870, Langdell was determined to reform the way Harvard educated future lawyers. Like many law schools, Harvard's standards had declined along with state bar requirements. By 1869, Harvard had reduced schooling to 18 months and dropped examinations. The latter were considered undignified; students were gentlemen and a gentleman's word that he considered himself proficient to practice law was thought to be good enough.

Langdell immediately strengthened the curriculum by reintroducing examinations—against loud student and faculty

57

protest—and extending the required term to two years, while encouraging three. He took a catalog of courses emphasizing legal theory that had not changed in 25 years and junked it for a curriculum heavy on legal methods and practice. Courses in the theory of jurisprudence were dropped; courses on civil procedure and criminal law became requirements.

But Langdell's most significant and controversial reforms focused on the way law was taught. The old method of teaching at Harvard and elsewhere was simple and not particularly effective for the real world of legal practice. Professors lectured, students listened, and quizzes were given to make sure the students had memorized the lists of legal rules drawn up by the professors.

This illustration captures the informality of a trial in the western territories, where unlettered Americans struggled to bring justice to the frontier. Though a shootout might be dramatic, more commonly prosecutions were for cutting timber on government property, stealing mail, or robbing army posts.

Langdell abandoned this method with his very first class. He never asked his students to memorize legal theories or rules, and he even dropped the lecture format. Instead, Langdell introduced the case method, a technique employed by law schools to this day. This new style of teaching law emphasized practice. Langdell had his students read reported cases and come to class prepared to state the facts and argue for the plaintiff and the defendant. He then grilled them, employing a string of questions and answers known as the Socratic method of teaching, named after the ancient Greek philosopher-teacher.

The case method got students to think on their feet and to focus on what lawyers were supposed to do: win their clients' cases. The case method also disturbed the settled ways of the Harvard Law School. Students and faculty complained. They were used to thinking about the law as something theoretical, almost eternal. Langdell was teaching law as something practical and changeable—law as a science.

Enrollment quickly declined, but Langdell and Harvard president Charles Eliot stuck to their guns. It took over ten years—enough time for some of Langdell's students to show their stuff in court—for things to turn around. By the 1880s, enrollment at Harvard was soaring and, by the first decades of the 20th century, most of the nation's law schools had adopted Langdell's case method of teaching.

At the same time, law schools adopted Langdell's other reforms. By 1920, nearly every law school had adopted Harvard's core curriculum of tort, contract, civil procedure, criminal, real property, evidence, and equity law. The three-year program became standard, and by 1907 many schools were using full-time law professors rather than practicing lawyers.

A representative of the Working Women's Protective Union serves as counsel for a young sewing machine operator at a disciplinary hearing in 1874. Women's rights began to be recognized in law toward the end of the 19th century. Early laws did not give married women legal equality if they came to a marriage with property, which became their husband's. By the 1840s, a number of states had modified those laws. In New York State, married women obtained the right not only to control their property and assets but to control the increase in those assets after marriage through business, trade, labor, or services. In the Dakotas, women held one-third of the land by 1886, and by the turn of the century women made up nearly 15 percent of western homesteaders.

Despite these changes, legal education was still lax in much of the country. Law schools were opening up coast to coast, offering day and evening courses for working-class and immigrant students. Some of these schools were solid, and some were not. However, each one emphasized a very practical approach, without the frills of legal theory and without courses in the more obscure branches of the law.

The changes in legal education both reflected and spurred on changes in the legal profession. For one thing, the growth in law

This early cartoon points out the double standard in the administration of justice between the rich and the poor.

A scene from the trial of a group of anarchists in Chicago in 1886, one of the most unfair trials in American history. An unidentified individual had thrown a bomb into Haymarket Square, where striking workers of the McCormick Harvester Company had gathered to protest police harassment. The bomb killed 7 policemen and injured 67 others. The police had already killed 4 strikers the day before the incident. The two unions involved, the American Federation of Labor and the Knights of Labor, were blameless, but Chicago was viewed as a hotbed of radicalism and the frightened public needed a scapegoat. Eight anarchists were rounded up and charged with murder on the grounds that they incited the bomb thrower. There was no evidence to link the 8 men to the crime, but they were found guilty. One received a prison sentence and the other 7 were sentenced to death.

schools meant more lawyers. Before the Civil War, there were less than 25,000 practicing lawyers in the United States. By 1900, there were over 100,000.

This growth in numbers did not always translate into professional bigness. Throughout the 19th century, most law firms were two-man operations, consisting of a courthouse lawyer with a good speaking style and an ability to think on his feet, and a documents man who prepared the growing paperwork connected with the cases.

Of course, the growth of corporations in the late 19th century spurred the development of larger law firms like the Cravath firm or the offices of Thomas Shearman and John Sterling. These Wall Street firms specialized in corporate mergers, bond issues, and stockholder suits. Clerks and secretaries were hired to handle paperwork, and associate lawyers were put on the payroll to handle the details of major cases.

In 1885, the Prudential Insurance Company retained the "exclusive attention" of its attorneys and the concept of in-house counsel was born. Whether in-house or independent, Wall Street lawyers emphasized conservative lawyering. The Wall Street firm, one historian has written, "did not feed on lawsuits, rather it avoided them."

The growing importance of corporate lawyers was reflected in their personal careers. A number of judges left the bench to become in-house counselors for the railroads. Kansas chief justice Albert Horton resigned his seat to work for the Missouri Pacific in 1895, while G. W. McCrary left the federal bench to represent the Santa Fe Railroad. Careers followed the opposite path as well. Both the Northern Pacific and the New York Central railroads came to be run by their former in-house lawyers.

A court scene in the Lizzie Borden murder trial. Lizzie Borden, the daughter of a prosperous Fall River, Massachusetts, businessman, was accused of murdering her father and stepmother with an ax in 1892. Although she was acquitted, Borden was shunned by the Fall River community. The murder weapon was found on the family property after she died. One theory was that when her father threatened to change his will and leave his property to his wife, Borden became enraged and killed them both. It was one of the most sensational cases of its time.

Judges and lawyers going to court through the western woodlands. Judges and lawyers often carried guns and knives in the early days of the frontier, when court sessions were held in log houses or saloons and anything could happen.

The late 19th century was not just a time of corporate and industrial growth; it was also an age of corruption. State and federal legislators, many of whom were practicing lawyers, openly took bribes by railroads and other corporations. The great industrial magnates also used the courts to do their bidding. They got judges to throw injunctions at striking workers and at other corporations. In New York City, where many of the corporations were headquartered and where the political scene was dominated by the corrupt Tammany machine (a group of corrupt politicians), judges like George Barnard and Albert Cardozo offered their services to the highest corporate bidder.

In 1870, after a particularly vicious corporate battle involving the Erie Railroad—where one of the lawyers was actually beaten and hospitalized—a number of prominent lawyers decided to take action to clean up the profession. They formed the Association of the Bar of the City of New York. By year's end, the association had about 450 mostly prosperous business lawyers as members—the "decent part" of the profession. Between 1870 and 1878, 16 more bar associations were founded in 12 states, culminating in the formation of the American Bar Association (ABA) in 1878.

Like many of the other professional organizations formed at this time, the ABA had two interconnected goals. First, it wanted to clean up the profession and improve its public image. At the same time, it wanted to limit competition and restrict its ranks. This second goal was pursued in the name of the first. By making the profession more exclusive, the ABA could claim it was weeding out potentially corrupt and unprofessional members. But oftentimes, limiting entry into the profession meant keeping out immigrants, the working class, and blacks. It also meant keeping out price-cutters and low-budget law offices.

The ABA and the bar associations went after law schools, offering accreditation to those institutions that met their standards and threatening to withhold accreditation to those schools that failed to raise theirs. Schools that failed to get accredited were hard-pressed to recruit students. These, of course, were not the major university-affiliated law schools, but the small and inexpensive night schools.

However, the bar association directed its main efforts at the admissions process. The problem, they said, was simple. It was too easy to become a lawyer. In 1890, only 16 out of 49 states and territories controlled admission to the bar through a single agency or court. And those that did gave only a cursory examination. One lawyer described his 1877 "examination" in Tennessee as shaking hands with the judge and showing him his law school diploma. By passing the bar in Tennessee, he could practice law in most other states as well. In fact, many states granted law school graduates diploma privilege, that is, potential lawyers were automatically allowed to pass the bar and practice law with a degree from any law school, accredited or not, in the state.

Association members—usually graduates of the more prestigious schools—resented the lax rules and the upstart schools. They wanted stricter requirements and tougher examinations. In New York and other states, they got legislatures to repeal diploma privilege and reinstate bar examinations. By the turn of the century, New York and a host of other states had set up central examining boards of skilled lawyers to control admission to the bar.

The Law and Social Change

GOVERNMENTS, THOMAS JEFFERSON WROTE IN THE
Declaration of Independence, are instituted to secure mankind's
"inalienable rights . . . [to] life, liberty, and the pursuit of happiness."
In American history, that has included two important missions:
keeping the peace among citizens, through penal codes and
punishment, and protecting the helpless.

Both aims, however, involved fundamental questions about what
kind of country America would be. With the legacy of a revolution
against English tyranny, Americans tried to enforce public order and
safety without creating a new national tyranny. The Bill of Rights
included, among other things, the right to fair and speedy trials and
protection from "cruel and unusual" punishment.

As for protecting the needy and helpless, Americans have tried to
balance their charitable and humanitarian impulses with the belief
that, in a land of opportunity, everyone can and should stand on
their own two feet. In the two centuries since independence, the

A late-19th-century policeman on his post. Philadelphia hired its first paid constables in 1833. Boston established a salaried day force of six men in 1838, and New York formed a police force in 1845 modeled on London's Metropolitan Police.

government's approach to punishment and protection has evolved as an ever-changing balance of these different forces.

At the time of the Revolution, poor relief was usually local. Orphans, widows, the disabled, and paupers took room and board with families who received government compensation for their efforts. In the few urban areas, food and clothing were distributed as "outdoor relief." Criminals were punished by terms in local jails, fines, whippings, or the public humiliation of being placed in stocks.

During the "age of reform," from the 1820s to the 1840s, attitudes about the helpless and the criminal changed. Increasingly, both were seen as victims of moral decay and weakness, who could be reformed with the right care. Along with these changing attitudes

The faces of juvenile delinquents. Julia Lathrop, a Hull House worker in Chicago, helped to establish the country's first juvenile court in that city in 1899. By 1904, all but three of the states had such courts. The juvenile was not judged by his act but by his character, background, and home life. Some youngsters were sent to rehabilitative institutions, but probation was the preferred solution, with a probation officer assigned to work with the child after his release into the community. Before such courts were established, youthful offenders were more likely simply to be thrown into city prisons.

came changing responses. Outdoor relief for the poor was replaced by indoor relief—poorhouses and orphanages where the recipients could learn work habits and self-discipline. Under the relentless pressure of reformer Dorothea Dix, the insane were removed from jails and placed in new asylums, built and operated specifically for that purpose.

As for punishment, penal codes were modified. The codification of criminal laws increasingly replaced the unwritten body of common law crimes, which dated back to English precedent and were often arbitrarily imposed by judges. Among the new codes was a recognition of degrees of murder and a narrowing of the number of crimes for which the death penalty was imposed. In South Carolina, that number decreased from 165 in 1813 to 22 in 1850. In Michigan and Wisconsin, the penalty was done away with altogether by 1848.

At the same time, states throughout the Midwest and Northeast embarked on a penitentiary building campaign. Designed to replace the dirty and crowded urban jails, the new penitentiaries, such as Auburn in New York and Pennsylvania's Eastern State, were designed to do more than incarcerate criminals. They were intended to rehabilitate them. A strict educational, religious, and work regimen was supposed to turn the inmate away from a life of crime. To keep bad influences to a minimum, inmates were kept apart; to get the prisoners to reflect on their evil ways, talking was prohibited.

While proponents said the penitentiaries—derived from the word penitence—offered criminals a new chance on life, some observers felt the silence and isolation was actually more inhumane than whipping or a stay in an overcrowded urban jail. On a visit to a Pennsylvania penitentiary in 1842, English novelist Charles Dickens wrote of the "slow and daily tampering with the mysteries of the brain . . . immeasurably worse than any torture of the body."

The decades following the Civil War—the so-called Gilded Age—witnessed government's retreat from penal reform and charity. Increasingly, the public's attitude toward the criminal changed. No longer was he seen as a victim of a poor moral upbringing but as the inheritor of innate criminal traits. Both popular magazines and scholarly journals published articles about the physical appearance of criminals. Among other things, thin beards, long arms, and stooping shoulders were signs of the "criminal type." Skulls were measured for bumps indicating a propensity for criminal behavior. In this reactionary atmosphere, support for the penitentiary evaporated. Strict reform regimens were replaced by harsh punishment.

Despite the decline of reform, several innovations in the penal codes and punishment did emerge in the late 19th century.

(continued on page 75)

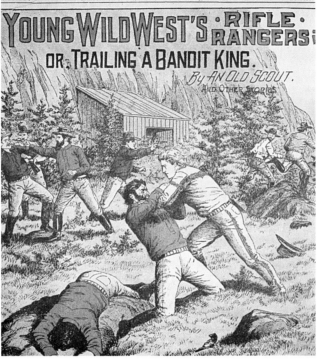

The front cover of an early dime novel of the type that romanticized the exploits of western frontiersmen, gunslingers, bandits, and lawmen. Much of our misinformation about the West came from such sensationalized accounts.

At Fourth Avenue and 15th Street in New York City in the 1870s, a police officer holds back horse traffic so that children may cross the street. The quaintness of the illustration belies the fact that such streets were dangerous and many fatal accidents were caused by the bustling carriages and wagons.

In 1912, suffragettes march in New York City to demand the right of women to vote and participate in political life. Before World War I, a number of individual states had granted women the right to vote, but full suffrage for women did not come until after the war.

(continued from page 70)

These included indeterminate and suspended sentencing. Indeterminate sentencing permitted time off for good behavior in prison. Suspended sentencing, first attempted in New York in 1894, allowed the judge to forego the entire sentence if there were "mitigating circumstances."

All of these new approaches led to another new idea: parole. The history of parole began in the 1840s when John Augustus, a Boston bootmaker who liked to visit the courts, began bailing out men he saw convicted for crimes they committed when drunk or in desperation. The judges, impressed by his charity and its positive results, often waived imprisonment and placed the criminals in the care of Augustus. By the time he died in 1859, Augustus had paroled almost 2,000 criminals. In 1878, Massachusetts appointed a paid probation officer to serve Boston. In 1891, the idea was expanded statewide and, within 10 years, Missouri, Vermont, Rhode Island, and New Jersey had followed suit.

Juvenile justice was another goal of Gilded Age reform. In 1870, New York established a new "reformatory" for juvenile offenders between 16 and 30 "not known to have been previously sentenced to a State prison." The old reform ideas were now applied to the young only. Given indeterminate sentences, they were taught trades and religious instruction. Prisoners were divided into various "classes." Good behavior moved a prisoner up to a higher class with more privileges. From the highest class, a prisoner might be paroled.

Despite these limited reforms, the Gilded Age was not known as a particularly humanitarian age, especially in its attitudes toward the poor. The late 19th century was a time of growing disparities in wealth, a volatile business cycle, and periods of high unemployment. Americans naturally wondered why there was so much financial hurt

The 19th-century horse-drawn police patrol wagon was known as the Black Maria because of its resemblance to the hearses of the time.

Children in a city prison in the 1870s. Before the establishment of juvenile courts, juvenile offenders could be tried and sent to prison as adults. In 1870, Massachusetts recorded more than 2,000 minors in jail, with 10 percent under 15 years of age.

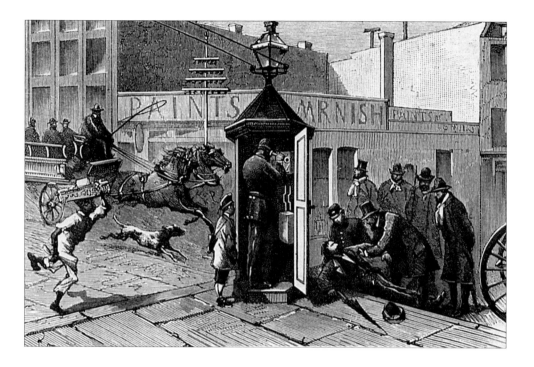

In 1882, police in Chicago set up the first police call box.

in a land of plenty. The answer, for many, came from the realm of science, more specifically from the evolutionary theories of Charles Darwin.

The theory of "social Darwinism" was simplicity itself. According to its proponents, including the English philosopher Herbert Spencer and the Yale professor William Graham Sumner, the natural force of "survival of the fittest" applied to human society. The rich were rich because they were smarter, more disciplined, and better adapted to the rapid changes of industrial society. And the poor? Well, they were not. As for government aid to the poor and private charity, it simply

77

Prisoners returning from work assignment at the prison on Blackwell's Island in New York City. Overall, early prisons were terribly managed and underfunded. Those who ran them were often appointed as a way to pay off political debts.

promoted the reproduction of the weakest and least adaptable members of the species.

With the dawn of the 20th century, however, many Americans began to recognize that the individualist philosophy of the past no longer worked. With the massive influx of immigrants—almost nine million in the first decade of the new century—and the equally substantial movement off the land by rural Americans, the nation was growing more urbanized. For example, between 1870 and 1910, Chicago burned to the ground, was rebuilt, and multiplied its population seven times. But big cities meant big social problems. The old individualist philosophy was inevitably replaced by a new interdependent one. The "Progressive Era" was born.

Progressives came from so many different backgrounds and tried to solve so many different social problems that it is hard to find one definition that fits all. But Progressives did share several ideas about human society. First, they discarded the 19th-century notion that society was guided by absolute and unvarying rules and that scientists merely discovered them the way they discovered principles of nature or physics.

Progressives argued that societies change and that these changes must be studied by direct experience. This included the law. As Oliver Wendell Holmes, Supreme Court justice from 1902 to 1932, wrote, "the life of the law has not been logic; it has been experience." Even more importantly, Progressives believed that the social environment could be changed for the better. Man, argued sociologist Lester Ward, could "shape environmental forces to his own advantage . . . [through] rational planning and social engineering." Criminal behavior was the result of social environment, Progressives argued. And if the social environment could be improved, then the source of crime would be eliminated. Harvard Law School dean

"Tenement Alley," one of the toughest sections of New York City along Mulberry Street, as captured by social reformer and photojournalist Jacob Riis. Such neighborhoods were breeding grounds for criminals. Riis, the son of a Danish schoolteacher, had lived in this area before he was assigned to cover it as a police reporter for the *New York Sun*. Riis captured the misery of tenement dwellers in his book *How the Other Half Lives*, published in 1890.

Boston police around 1920 show off their latest weapon, a motorized machine gun carrier that was used to quell May Day riots in the city.

Roscoe Pound called for "sociological jurisprudence," which meant "the adjustment of principles and doctrines to the human conditions they are to govern rather than assumed first principles."

Many Progressives found their inspiration in religion. The "social gospel," as it was labeled by its most influential proponents, Congregational minister Washington Gladden of Columbus, Ohio, and Baptist minister Walter Rauschenbusch of Rochester, New York, asked churches to reassert the "social aims of Jesus." The "kingdom of God on Earth," he argued, "could not be won by personal salvation alone, but through the struggle for social justice." Rauschenbusch's call for a social gospel led to the foundation of the Federal Council of Churches in 1908, an organization dedicated to "promoting the application of the law of Christ in every relation to human life."

Gladden and Rauschenbusch's ideas awakened the social conscience of many young people, including settlement house founders Jane Addams and Lillian Wald. First developed in England, settlement houses were established in many large American cities. Providing health care, art and sports programs, education in civics, and English instruction, the settlement houses tried to help immigrants and other inhabitants of the city's slums and ghettos adjust to urban life. Settlement houses, like Addams's Hull House in Chicago and Wald's Henry Street Settlement in New York City, dedicated themselves to Americanizing immigrants, especially the young, even at the cost of abandoning native cultures that some Progressives called backward, undemocratic, and criminally inclined.

For good and for bad, settlement houses provided services that municipal governments did not. But the founders of the houses and other practitioners of the social gospel did not stop there; they advocated broader reforms as well. Improved public education, they felt, would help immigrant children adjust to American life better

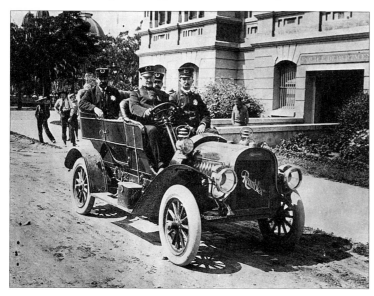

In 1907, police in San Jose, California, began to use motorized patrol cars. The automobile's utility for police work was recognized almost as soon as it was invented, and the horse-drawn paddy wagon quickly disappeared.

81

than Catholic and other parochial schools of the inner city. In this struggle to push public education, the reformers ran up against immigrant groups determined to preserve religious education.

An even bigger fight occurred over alcohol. Social gospelers believed that one of the major sources of crime and poverty was the bottle. It destroyed individuals and contributed to a violent and immoral climate that infected the young. Women reformers were particularly active since they saw alcohol as a destroyer of marriages and home life. During the 1880s and the 1890s, the Women's Christian Temperance Union and the Anti-Saloon League organized branches in every major city in America. Their goal: ban the saloon.

Indeed, American cities at the turn of the century were awash in saloons. In many districts of Chicago, for instance, there was nearly one saloon for every 100 men, women, and children. And, as reformers argued, saloons bred other vices like gambling and prostitution. On the other hand, the saloon was often the only public place in immigrant ghettos and the center of working-class politics. The political machines that ran most of America's cities used the saloons as informal offices where the local politicians—known as ward heelers—offered jobs and services for votes and money. Machine politicians and immigrant spokespersons argued that the antisaloon campaign was really an anti-immigrant crusade.

Despite the criticism, the reformers proceeded. They spread pamphlets and developed public school programs. Some, like Carry Nation, turned to direct action, invading saloons and smashing the liquor barrels with axes. More effective, however, were their political efforts. They got cities to pass option rules, allowing individual city wards to vote for a "dry," or anti-alcohol, option. In Chicago, they were successful enough to ban alcohol in almost half the city's

A large number of police vans lined up in front of police headquarters in New York City in 1935. The picture was taken shortly before a massive raid on Central Park that resulted in the arrest of close to 400 people suspected of beating and robbing innocent strollers at night.

districts by 1908, although most of these were in the nonimmigrant outer neighborhoods. Finally, they triumphed in 1919 with the Eighteenth Amendment, which banned alcohol throughout the United States.

Many Progressives understood, however, that banning alcohol was not enough to create the kind of social environment that would Americanize immigrants, reduce poverty, and eliminate crime. Positive efforts were needed as well, and that meant reforming the political process. Between 1902 and 1903, Lincoln Steffens, a "muckraking" investigative journalist, wrote a series of exposés on big city corruption for *McClure's* magazine, a popular middle-class monthly. Steffens and other reformers attacked political machines like Tammany Hall in New York City, criminal organizations that shook down small businesses for protection money, extorted bribes from companies trying to do business with the city, and offered lucrative city contracts to political cronies. In many cities, such as Detroit, Toledo, and Cleveland, the efforts to replace the machines with "good government" administrations were successful. In the bigger cities, it took longer. Tammany Hall's grip on power was not broken until the 1930s and the election of reformer Fiorello LaGuardia.

Once in power, the reformers attempted to institutionalize the efforts of settlement houses and the social gospelers and extend them to the entire city. They enjoyed broad popular support. The public's concern had been raised by exposés of poverty beginning in 1890 with the publication of Jacob Riis's book *How the Other Half Lives*, with its powerful photos of the urban slums.

Like settlement house workers, reform politicians believed that improving the urban environment would reduce poverty, immorality, and crime. And to improve the urban environment, the corrupt politics of the machine era would have to be replaced by the efficiency of the social sciences. Experts were brought in to reform city housing, parks, education, utilities, and other services. A "city beautiful" movement emerged with its agenda for the planned city. One of its biggest boosters, Chicago architect Daniel Burnham, helped lay out postfire Chicago, postearthquake San Francisco, and turn-of-the-century Washington with extensive parks, broad boulevards, and impressive public monuments. Burnham's motto: "make no small plans."

In most cities, however, the changes in the urban environment were less grandiose, though the social engineering was not. In the belief that decent housing assured physical and mental health, new tenement laws—like New York's pioneering 1901 statute requiring indoor toilets, fire safeguards, and more light and air between buildings—were enacted. With studies showing that physical exercise helped turn children away from vice and crime, public playgrounds and parks were carved out of crowded immigrant neighborhoods.

Workplace conditions—especially for women and children—became the concern of reformer Josephine Shaw Lowell. Declaring that "if the working people had all they ought to have, we should not have the paupers and criminals," Shaw established the New York Consumers League in 1890. The League's most important effort was the "white list," a consumer's guide to businesses that treated their employees fairly. Under the leadership of Florence Kelley, a factory inspector from Illinois, the movement went national.

Relying on the data the League collected, the Supreme Court held in its 1908 *Muller* decision that an Oregon law limiting the workday

In 1932, two New York City police officers learn to use their new radio-equipped patrol cars.

for women to 10 hours was both constitutional and necessary for the health of American women. The decision was a landmark since it was the first time the Supreme Court had modified—in the public interest—its individualist philosophy that all workers and all

employers should be able to agree to any working conditions
they pleased.

As is often the case, the reform cause was furthered by tragedy.
On March 25, 1911, a fire in the Triangle Shirtwaist Factory killed
146 workers, mostly women and girls who burned to death behind
locked doors or jumped from the high-rise windows.

In the wake of the fire and the national outrage it produced, a State
Factory Commission was established. Within four years, New York
had over 56 laws dealing with fire hazards, unsafe machinery, and
conditions of home employment.

Some Progressives took their efforts of improving the social
environment to the national government. With the succession of
Theodore Roosevelt to the presidency in 1901 (upon the assassination
of William McKinley), the reformers had a sympathetic ear in the
White House. Launching his "square deal" in 1904, Roosevelt sought
to use the powers of the federal government to curb the abuses of big
business. Under Roosevelt, the Food and Drug Administration—with
its mandate to protect the public against dangerous drugs and
unhealthful food—was established in 1906.

Other reforms were taken up by Woodrow Wilson, a Democrat
elected to the presidency in 1912. Under Wilson, a workmen's
compensation act, a federal child labor law, and a statute limiting
railroad workers to an eight-hour workday were all put into effect.
Even the income tax amendment, added to the Constitution in 1913,
was seen as progressive since it was originally designed to finance
social reform by taxing the wealthy.

The United States's entry into World War I in 1917 slowed
progressive efforts dramatically. The government pulled away from
its mission to reform society in its effort to win the war. Instead of

curbing the power of big business, the national government expanded it by throwing huge war contracts its way.

Immigrants experienced wartime hysteria against foreigners. In 1921 and 1924, Congress passed two immigration bills that effectively cut off all immigration except from a few select countries such as Britain, Ireland, and Germany.

The Law and the Frontier

THE WORLD CAME TO CHICAGO IN 1893, TO THE WORLD Columbian Exposition erected on the swampland of the city's South Side. Officially, the fair commemorated the 400th anniversary of America's "discovery." Unofficially, the exposition offered a spectacular showcase for a nation on the threshold of industrial supremacy and world power.

Among the fair's lesser-heralded attractions was a lecture delivered by a young historian named Frederick Jackson Turner. Like the fair, the lecture, entitled "The Significance of the Frontier in American History," looked backward even as it assessed the future. Turner's now-famous thesis was that the frontier was central to American history and civilization.

According to Turner, the frontier had shaped the nation's identity, its people, its institutions, and its laws. The wide-open politics of the frontier had constantly challenged the antidemocratic—even "aristocratic"—tendencies of the long-settled East. It had also prevented European-style radicalism and socialism, he argued,

Farmers attend a meeting of the National Grange in 1873. The Grange was founded in the 1860s as a social and self-help organization for farmers. When the depression of 1873 caused farm prices to fall, the Grange became political and began to fight the railroad monopolies for fairer freight rates and the banks and government for easier credit policies.

because it operated as a "safety valve," offering land to workers who might become discontented with shrinking opportunities in the East.

Moreover, Turner noted, because men and women had been going out West to seek their fortunes, often with little more than muscle and hope, the frontier had been the source of American egalitarianism. There the nation's emphasis on individualism and enterprise had been validated with each pioneer's struggle against a hostile environment. And finally, said Turner, the frontier had been the source of America's distinct political and legal system. The rough-and-tumble frontier spurred a more pragmatic approach to legal issues. The lack of established government and law encouraged more popular forms of justice, while the new and varied environment helped America wean itself from English law and establish legal codes and procedures of its own.

A vigilance court in session in the Far West. In the northern and western states, farmers and small ranchers were in the majority, and they elected the county sheriffs and local judges and determined how the law would be applied. A rustler, accused by a rich cattle baron, was rarely convicted in spite of the evidence. Juries on the whole were sympathetic to the common man struggling to make a living, even if not quite legally. The cattle barons, on the other hand, were known to refuse the demands of the cowboys for higher pay. They enclosed lands and sources of water with barbed wire and left smaller ranchers to fend for themselves. If the wealthy ranchers could not get satisfaction from the courts, they would often hire vigilante groups to deal with their enemies.

A vigilante group hangs an alleged murderer in 1888. The vigilantes were little better than mobs or private armies of gunmen, but sometimes they were motivated by social reform. California had 27 vigilance committees in the 1850s, mostly directing their activities against corrupt local government. If local governments were too inept or too slow to address problems, the vigilantes would take matters into their own hands.

But, Turner said, all that was passing. According to the U.S. Census for 1890, the frontier was no more. The American people had settled the entire continent—except for a few remaining pockets of open territory—from the Atlantic to the Pacific. And Turner worried that the end of the frontier would dry up the fount of America's unique greatness. America needed a new frontier, and overseas territories, he prophesied, would be it.

Like all great theories, Turner's frontier thesis of American history had a long incubation period. The nation's founding fathers also saw the frontier as America's future. Before they even wrote the Constitution, they established a system whereby western territories would be incorporated into the Union on an equal basis with established states. Passed in 1787, the Northwest Ordinance first applied to the Old Northwest of the Great Lakes region, but it was later used as a precedent for settling most of the territories west of the Appalachian Mountains. Among other things, the Ordinance established a three-stage process for legal statehood, thus assuring that the American frontier would be an equal partner in the nation's democracy rather than a vast interior colony.

First, until the white male population (blacks did not count as citizens until 1867 and women even later) reached 5,000, lawmaking power was vested in a presidentially appointed governor and three federal judges. But, according to the Ordinance, these officials could only "adopt and publish" laws. That is, they could only borrow laws off the books of established states. Naturally enough, most territorial officials borrowed from the states they came from.

Partial exceptions to the importation of eastern law included states where older civil law had been established by the Spanish or French. For many years, remnants of civil law coexisted with the common law tradition imported by American settlers in states like California, New Mexico, Texas, and, especially, Louisiana.

In the second stage, after the white male population reached 5,000, lawmaking authority was both expanded to include the writing of new law (so long as it was "not repugnant" to the Ordinance) and was shared between a federally appointed governor and a legislature divided between locally elected representatives and federal appointees. The third stage, or statehood, was achieved when the white male population reached 60,000.

The combined courthouse and saloon owned by Judge Roy Bean in Langtry, Texas, in 1900. Bean became famous for his harsh and sometimes bizarre judgments. He once fined a dead man $40 for carrying a concealed weapon.

Black soldiers of the 25th U.S. Infantry Regiment stand at attention outside their barracks at Fort Randall, Dakota Territory, in 1880. Four regiments of black soldiers were stationed on the Great Plains after the Civil War. They were tough soldiers who were praised by their commander, General William Tecumseh Sherman, and respected by the Apache they fought.

Equally important were the Ordinance's economic elements. Of all the things Americans sought on the frontier, the most important was land. The Ordinance required all lands to be sold in fee simple. That is, the owner had the right to do with his land as he wished, thus assuring a growing free market where lands could be bought and sold freely. But this policy also encouraged speculation (buying and selling to make a profit from changing prices), especially since much of the land was sold in blocs that favored large-scale investors.

This trend continued after the Civil War in the settlement of lands west of the Mississippi River. Many western territories, for example, had lenient adverse possession laws. That is, people who had lived on and improved land that was subject to dispute with an absentee landowner would most likely be awarded the land. While in the eastern states, the length of time a settler had to be on the land was usually 20 years, in western states like Nevada it was reduced to 5.

Still, most western territories and states required the occupying party to show proof that they had been paying taxes on the land all along. This was meant to discourage squatters and demonstrate that the occupiers legitimately held claim to the land.

Even more encouraging to the settlement of western lands was the Homestead Act, passed by Congress in 1862. The act's provisions were simple enough. Heads of families—including unmarried women and immigrants who had taken out naturalization papers—were eligible to receive 160 free acres of land after five years of settlement.

But, like the earlier land arrangements of the Old Northwest, the land deals under the Homestead Act often favored wealthy speculators and developers. For instance, a provision in the act allowed homesteaders to buy the land at a minimum price, usually $1.25 an acre, before the five years was up. Between 1881 and 1904, 22 million acres or about one-fourth of homesteaded land was paid off in this way. As a Senate report stated, "not one in a hundred" of these commuted lands was "ever occupied as a home . . . They became part of some large timber holding or a parcel of a cattle or sheep ranch."

In fact, most of the best land in the western territories was not even available under the Homestead Act. States entering the Union were given a "dowry" of land from the federal government, plus land reserved for land-grant colleges. States then sold this land to the highest bidder, oftentimes in large blocs to real estate promoters who then sold it to individual farmers.

Much of the best land went to the railroads. The government recognized that better transportation was the key to opening up the western territories. But unlike the canal-building era before the Civil War—when state governments often did the construction themselves—the postwar period emphasized private development.

Beginning gradually in the 1850s, but expanding rapidly after the Civil War, the federal and state governments gave over 150 million acres to railroads to encourage construction. Government grants of land to the railroads usually included exclusive ownership of the right of way plus alternating plots to a distance of 5 to 20 miles from the track. Since the land granted lay next to the railroad tracks, it was by definition the most valuable real estate in the territory.

Two other legal problems complicated the picture of western settlement. The first problem emerged out of the war the United States provoked with Mexico in 1846. In the Treaty of Guadalupe Hidalgo that ended the war in 1848, the United States took possession of large tracts of western territory. At the same time, the

The last Native American group to resist the white man were the Apache bands led by Geronimo, pictured here on the right with three of his warriors. When the Apache chief Cochise died in 1874, Geronimo refused to honor what he perceived as an unfair treaty with the American government. With a small group of followers, he fought on for another 10 years. After his band had been reduced to no more than 30 people, including women and children, he surrendered in 1886.

United States promised to uphold land claims and honor existing civil codes originally established in those territories by the Mexican government (and Mexico's colonial ruler until 1810, Spain).

In California, a class of Mexican ranchers known as Californios owned large tracts of land throughout the territory. But the gold rush of 1849 and the vast influx of Anglo-Americans overwhelmed the Mexican population and led to illegal seizures of land. Californios could sue in court, but the procedure was long and expensive. In northern California, where the vast majority of Anglos settled, Mexicans lost their claims to most of the land within a generation. In slower-growing southern California, the displacement was largely completed by 1900, though people like the Dominguez family of the Los Angeles basin held onto their land well into the 20th century.

In New Mexico, where Anglo settlement proceeded more slowly and the Mexican population was far greater, the struggle over land was more drawn out. When Texas cattle ranchers forced their way onto territory known as the Las Vegas Grant in the 1880s and 1890s,

97

Mexican "pobres," or poor ones, abandoned the American courts and organized themselves into nightriding parties. Their long campaign of harassment against the Anglo invaders secured Mexican land ownership into the 20th century.

At the same time, however, the influx of Anglos saw the end of Mexican civil law, despite stipulations against such a development in the 1848 treaty. While a few odd bits survived here and there—such as community property laws in California and holographic, or nonwitnessed, wills in Texas—Mexican civil law, according to one legal historian, was simply "too alien and inaccessible to survive." When California entered the Union in 1850, the "common law of England" was made the "rule of decision in all the Courts of [the] State."

The second problem that complicated settlement was the very different climate and topography of the West. Across the 100th meridian—a line stretching from central Texas to the Dakotas—annual rainfall drops below 20 inches, making nonirrigated farming impossible. Water, abundant and free-flowing in the eastern states, was a rare and precious commodity in the Old West.

Laws concerning water rights had to change. The common law rule for water—established in rainy England and continued in the lusher districts of the eastern and southern United States—was based on riparian rights. That is, every landowner who fronted on a waterway had equal rights to the water, and no one could take so much that the supply was depleted.

But this made no sense along the tiny, seasonal gullies and arroyos of the West. Instead, a new doctrine was developed: prior appropriation or, essentially, a policy of first-come, first-served.

A rare photograph of Geronimo and his warriors. The Indians of the Plains—Apache, Sioux, Blackfeet, Cheyenne, Kiowa, Crow, and others—were mostly nomadic people who depended on the buffalo to sustain them. The army and private hunters destroyed the buffalo herds to starve the Indians out.

It recognized the fact that there would never be enough water to go around and it encouraged rapid development of the limited sources of water by assuring owners complete title to it. Prior appropriation became the rule of the land in most western states, though in Texas and California—with their dual wet-dry climate zones—old riparian rights coexisted alongside the western water codes.

Eventually, the federal and state governments would become involved in massive irrigation projects to supply the farmlands and cities of the West with a steady supply of water. By the turn of the century, the city of Los Angeles and the citrus growers of southern California had strong-armed the residents of the Owens Valley in the Sierra Nevada into damming up their valley. In northern California, naturalist John Muir, the founder of the Sierra Club, fought a losing battle in 1913 to preserve the Yosemite-like Hetch-Hetchy Gorge against a dam designed to supply water for the communities and farmers of the San Francisco Bay Area.

The lack of water in the West also meant a modification of homesteading rights. While a 160-acre farm made economic sense in

The Sioux chieftain Sitting Bull. When gold was discovered in the Black Hills of the Dakota Territory, prospectors and miners, with the encouragement of the army, began to invade sacred Indian lands guaranteed to the Sioux by the Treaty of Fort Laramie in 1868. Sitting Bull and Crazy Horse resisted, eventually gathering about 4,000 warriors to defeat George Armstrong Custer at the Battle of the Little Bighorn in 1876. Ironically, it was the Custer disaster that shocked the government into hunting down the last of the hostile tribes. Sitting Bull retreated into Canada for a time and was killed when he returned to South Dakota. Crazy Horse was murdered by army officers and Indian police after he surrendered.

In the 1880s, a new religion known as the Ghost Dance swept through depressed Native American communities. Whites feared that the religion would cause the Indians to leave their reservations in rebellion, and the government ordered an end to the religious ceremonies. In protest, a group of about 200 Indians, led by Chief Big Foot, assembled near Wounded Knee, South Dakota, to perform the Ghost Dance. They were tracked down, taken into custody, and then massacred by these soldiers of the 7th Cavalry in 1890.

the well-watered lands east of the 100th meridian, homestead holdings were expanded west of the line to much wider expanses. By common usage, ranchers had a "range right" to all the land between the rises on each side of the creeks they had homesteaded, areas that might encompass thousands of acres. Ranchers, in fact, treated the grasslands of Texas and the Great Plains as free public pasturage for their herds of cattle.

But as important as water was to the West, it was merely a means to other profitable ends, like farming and ranching. The vast mineral resources of the West, on the other hand, were a direct source of wealth and thus drew hundreds of thousands of settlers to California, Nevada, Colorado, Idaho, Montana, the Dakotas, and later Alaska.

Because mineral wealth was often concentrated in narrow zones and was discovered in an instant, its exploitation created overnight communities and instant law. Known as miners' codes, these laws were often drawn up, in the absence of legal authorities, by the miners themselves.

Beginning with the gold rush towns of California in 1849 and spreading later to diggings around Pikes Peak in Colorado in the 1850s and 1860s and the Black Hills of South Dakota in the 1870s, these codes focused on mining claims. They established rules for making claims, settling disputes among rival claimants, and enforcing decisions of miners' "courts." In California and elsewhere, laws were also passed to prevent Mexicans and other foreign miners like the Chinese from establishing new mining claims.

The legal irregularities of the frontier had their humorous side as well. In a hilarious vignette from the Comstock Lode of Nevada, Mark Twain described a "trespassing" case where the local "justices" had to adjudicate (act as judges) and decide rightful possession when a landslide laid one man's mountainside claim on top of his neighbor's claim below. "Gentlemen," Judge Referee Roop intoned, "it is the verdict of this court that the plaintiff . . . has been deprived of his ranch by the visitation of God!"

Eventually, as territories organized, judges sent from the East accepted many of the rules and procedures established by the miners' "courts." Rules established by the miners around Pikes Peak in 1859, for instance, were included in the territorial constitution of Colorado written up two years later. Moreover, the new territorial legislature validated the local claims and judgments rendered by the informal courts.

Miners or others whose legal claim to land was established by the provisional courts could even bring actions of trespass, ejectment, and forcible detainer in the territorial and state courts throughout the West. As one legal historian writes, the miners' courts and codes were part of an American tradition, a "makeshift judicial and political order, where settlement had run past borders of legitimate government."

A similar development occurred on the wagon trains rolling across the open country of the West. When Lafayette Tate murdered a man on the overland trail in 1852, a makeshift wagon train court—complete with judge, jury, and counsel—convicted, sentenced, and hanged the man.

A less glorious tradition of settlers taking the law into their own hands emerged in the West's first great metropolis, San Francisco. Like the mining towns and camps it served, San Francisco experienced explosive population growth in the years immediately following the discovery of gold in California. Within 12 years, the population soared from 812 to nearly 60,000. The government and courts left over from Mexican rule or established in the brief period of American occupation were overwhelmed by a population of transient gold-seekers from around the world and, more dangerous still, failed gold-seekers returning from the mining camps. Street crime was rampant, and government corruption undermined legal efforts to curb it.

In 1851 and 1856, a group of businessmen formed the San Francisco Vigilance Committees. Known as vigilantes, the committees defied local, state, and federal law enforcement. They sentenced and executed outlaws after perfunctory trials. While the movement died out in San Francisco with the establishment of better government law enforcement at the end of the 1850s, its legacy lived on elsewhere.

Wherever explosive population growth bred lawlessness, including Carson City, Nevada, in 1858 and Colorado and Montana in the 1860s, vigilantes took the law into their own hands. While some committees, like those in San Francisco, genuinely attempted to establish a rule of law where none existed, others, like the Carson City vigilantes, were simply groups challenging laws, social behavior, and individuals they did not like.

More lethal was the reign of "hanging" Judge Isaac Charles Parker, who served on the federal bench of Fort Smith, Arkansas, from 1875 to 1896. With his motto "Do equal and exact justice," Parker was the final legal authority for the Indian territory of Oklahoma, just west of Fort Smith. In his 21 years on the bench, Parker sentenced 160 men to be hanged, of which 79 were actually executed, including five members of the Rufus Buck gang hanged simultaneously from one gallows on July 1, 1896. The execution was attended by thousands, some of whom traveled hundreds of miles to see the unprecedented multiple execution.

FURTHER READING

American Social History Project Staff. *Who Built America? Working People and the Nation's Economy, Politics, Culture, and Society.* Vol. 2. New York: Pantheon, 1992.

Bakken, Gordon M. *The Development of Law on the Rocky Mountain Frontier: Civil Law & Society.* Westport, CT: Greenwood, 1983.

Blum, John M. *Republican Roosevelt.* 2nd ed. Cambridge, MA: Harvard University Press, 1977.

Dykstra, Robert R. *The Cattle Towns.* Lincoln: University of Nebraska Press, 1983.

Foner, Eric. *Reconstruction: America's Unfinished Revolution, 1863–1877.* New York: Harper & Row, 1989.

Friedman, Lawrence M. *A History of American Law.* 2nd ed. New York: Simon & Schuster, 1985.

Henretta, James, et al. *America's History.* 2nd ed. Chicago: Dorsey, 1993.

Horwitz, Morton J. *The Transformation of American Law, 1780–1860.* Cambridge, MA: Harvard University Press, 1979.

Hurst, J. Willard. *Law & the Conditions of Freedom in the Nineteenth-Century United States.* Madison: University of Wisconsin Press, 1964.

Hyman, Harold M., and William M. Wiecek. *Equal Justice Under Law.* New York: Harper & Row, 1982.

Limerick, Patricia. *The Legacy of Conquest: The Unbroken Past of the American West.* New York: Norton, 1988.

Nash, Gary B., and Julie R. Jeffrey. *The American People: Creating a Nation & a Society.* 2nd ed. New York: Harper & Row, 1990.

Seligman, Joel. *The High Citadel: The Influence of Harvard Law School.* Boston: Houghton Mifflin, 1978.

INDEX

PICTURE CREDITS

JAMES CIMENT studied American history at the City University of New York and has taught American history at the City College of New York for nine years. Formerly a writer for the history magazine *Search,* he is currently working on an encyclopedia of Native Americans.

Brass Padlock; size, 1¼-x1 inches.
Price, each.....14c
No. 13883. Eureka Brass Padlock; size, 1⅜-x1¼ inches.
Price, each.....15c
No. 13884. Eureka Brass Padlock; size, 2¼-...ches. Price, each.....18c
...885. Eureka Iron Padlock: size, 2⅜x1½ inches, each.....10c
...886. Eureka Iron Padlock; size, 3x2 inches, each.....12c

Wrought Iron Brass Bushed Padlock, solid brass wheel, side ward, double chamber, and double bitted keys. Extra fine finish.
No. 13887. Price, each.....15c
Per doz.....$1.55

...ght Iron Padlocks, brass ...e, double chamber, one ...ard revolving key pin, 2 bitted flat steel keys, fine
...888. Price, each.....25c
.....$2.75

Wrought Iron Tumbler Chain Padlocks, with brass bushing on back, self-locking, spring shackle with two flat double bitted steel keys, fine finish.
No. 13889. Price, each.....40c
Per doz.....$4.50
Solid Brass Padlocks, spring shackle, self-locking, plain finish, complete with two flat steel keys; size, 1¼ inches.
No. 13890. Price, each.....10c
Per doz.....$1.00

Cast bronze metal Padlocks, self-locking spring shackle. All inside work and springs are made of brass; extra quality and finish. Size, 2¼ inches; measurement includes shackle. Two flat steel keys.
No. 13891. Price, each, 12c; per doz.....$1.15

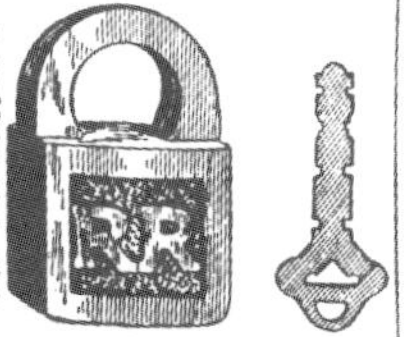

...lid bronze Padlocks. ...oof plun...ing shackle, ...king, double ...bolts. Best ...for the ...ever sold. ...hich in... shackle, ...892. Price, ...25c; per ...$2.85

Solid cast bronze metal Padlocks. Spring shackle, self-locking, all brass inside work, has 3 tumblers, etc. This lock has our latest improved dust-proof plunger; the instant shackle is withdrawn the opening is covered by a spring guard from the inside which keeps out all dirt, cinders, ashes, etc. We recommend them as a strictly high grade lock; one of the most durable locks made; also one of the most difficult locks to pick made. Complete with 2 keys. Price, each.....40c
Per doz.....$4.50
No. 13893. Same Lock as above, with 9 inch tinned chain. Price, each, 50c; per doz.....$5.00

houses, etc. A strictly high-grade lock and of the highest type of perfection in durability, workmanship and material. Nothing better made. Size, which includes shackle, 3½ inches, two keys furnished with each lock. Price, each, 60c; per doz. $7.00
No. 13894. Same lock as above with 10 inch japanned chain. Price, each, 75c; per doz.....$8.50

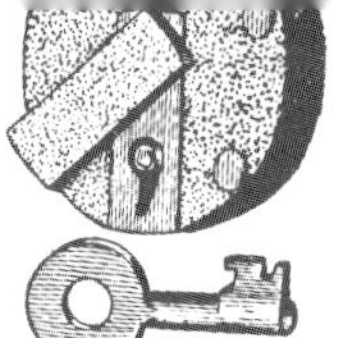

Lever Padlocks.

No. 13896. 6-Lever Padlocks are the finest, safest and most durable padlock sold at a reasonable price. Cast bronze outside. Brass inside. Phosphor bronze springs guaranteed not to rust or give out under the influence of any climate. Two nickel-plated flat steel keys with each lock. Size, 3½x2¼. Weight, 12 oz. Price, each.....85c
No. 13897. Same lock as above, with tinned iron chain attached. Price, each.....35c

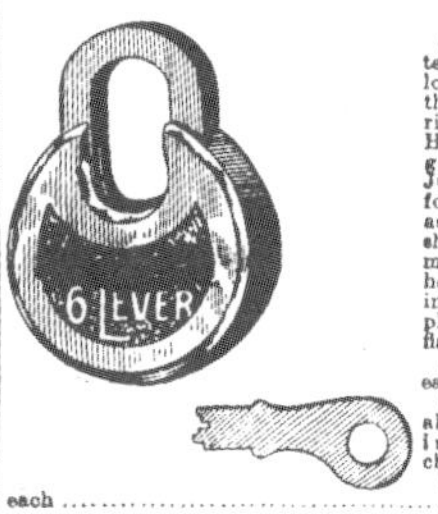

Special pattern 6-Lever Padlocks. Made of the same material as our 13896. Has heavy elongated shackle. Just the thing for gate or barn, as the long shackle will permit a chain or heavy staple being used. Complete, with two flat steel keys.
No. 13898. Price each.....40c
Same lock as above, with 9 inch tinned chain.
No. 13899. Price each.....50c

No. 13900. Nickel-Plated Brass Padlocks. Just the thing for small boxes, bags or dog collars. Size, 1⅛ inch. Price, each, 15c; per doz.....$1.75
No. 13901. 1¼ inch. Price, each 20c; per doz.....$2.15
No. 13902. 1½ inch. Price, each, 22c; per doz.....$2.40

Secure Lever Locks.

These locks cannot be picked except by a professional, and no key will unlock them unless it is like the original key. Each lock has two secure levers. We carry a full line of sizes. Note size carefully when ordering. Keys all different in a dozen.
No. 13925. Secure Lever Chest Lock. Double link, made of iron, size 1½x1¼ inches, key pin ½ inch from top of lock. Price, each, 20c; per doz.....$2.16
No. 13926. Secure Lever Chest Lock. Double link, made of iron, size 2x1⅝ inches, key pin ⅝ inch from top of lock. Price, each, 21c; per doz.....$2.32
No. 13927. Secure Lever Chest Lock. Double link, made of iron, size 2½x1⅝ inches, key pin ¾ inch from top of lock. Price, each, 22c; per doz.....$2.40
No. 13928. Secure Lever Chest Lock. Double link, made of iron, size 3x2 inches, key pin ⅞ inch from top of lock. Price, each, 26c; per doz.....$2.94
No. 13929. Secure Lever Chest Lock. Double link, made of iron, size 3½x2¼ inches, key pin 1 inch from top of lock. Price, each, 30c; per doz.....$3.42
No. 13930. Secure Lever Chest Lock. Double link, made of iron, size 4x2¾ inches, key pin 1¼ inches from top of lock. Price, each, 50c; per doz.....$5.37

...of any other concern will convince you there is a saving of from 25 per cent. to 45 per cent.

IN ORDERING SINGLE REVOLVERS WE ADVISE SENDING BY MAIL. This can be done where enough extra cent per oz., or fraction thereof. W... examination, on receipt of $1.00 as a guarantee of good faith. You can examine the revolver at the express... actly as represented, pay the express agent the balance and express charges and the revolver is yours. T... companies your order. We advise sending cash in full, deducting 3 per cent. for cash, and adding enough t... the revolver sent by mail.

Our 68c Revolver.

No. 876½ "Defender," wood stock, full nickel plated, plain cylinder, 7 shot, 22 caliber, rim fire, 2¼ inch barrel, weight 7 ounces. Safe and reliable. Each.....$0.68
Postage, extra, 10c.

Our 85c Revolver.

No. 877 Rosewood handle, 7 shot, full nickel plated, 22 caliber, long or short, rim fire, weight, 7 oz., 2¼ inch barrel, safe and reliable. Price.....$0.85
No. 877½ Rubber Handle, 7 shot, 22 caliber, long or short, rim fire, full nickel plated, weight 7 ounces, rifled barrel. Our special price.....$0.95

Defender, 32 Caliber.

No. 878. Rubber Handle, 5 shot, 32 caliber, rim fire, full nickel plated, weight 10 ounces, rifled barrel.
Our special price.....$1.20
Wood handle—same as above.
Our special price, each.....$0.85
For 10c extra we will send by open mail. For 18c extra we will send by registered mail.

Bull Dog Revolvers.

American Bull Dogs all double action, self-cocking; all have rubber stocks, all beautifully nickel plated; all have plated cylinders, all have octagon barrels, all warranted new and in perfect order. Regular retail price $3.00; our special price.....$1.35
Description: These revolvers are strictly first-class in every respect. The quality of material and workmanship is the best. All have rifled barrels and are good shooters; all 5 shot. These are not toys, but good guns. No one can meet our prices on these goods.

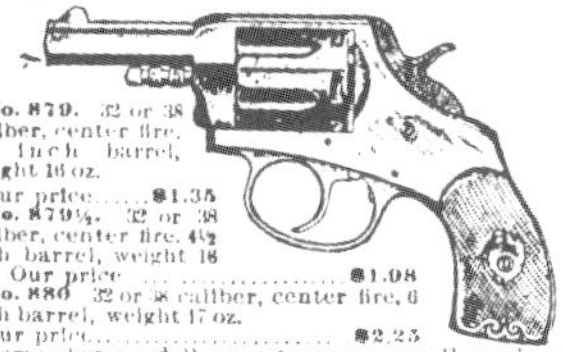

No. 879. 32 or 38 caliber, center fire, 2½ inch barrel, weight 16 oz.
Our price.....$1.35
No. 879½. 32 or 38 caliber, center fire, 4½ inch barrel, weight 18 oz. Our price.....$1.98
No. 880 32 or 38 caliber, center fire, 6 inch barrel, weight 17 oz.
Our price.....$2.25
Remember one dollar must accompany all revolver orders to be sent C. O. D., balance to be paid at express office. 3 per cent. discount if cash in full accompanies your order.
For 20c extra we will send by open mail, postpaid. For 28c extra we will send by registered mail, postpaid.
No. 880½ Rubber handle, 7 shot, 22 caliber, long or short, rim fire, full nickel plated, weight 7 oz., rifled barrel, price.....$1.35
Postage, extra, 10c.

Our $1.45 Revolver.

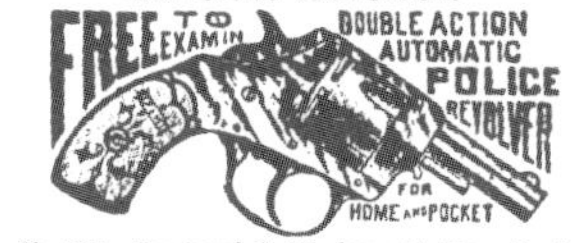
FREE TO EXAMIN
DOUBLE ACTION AUTOMATIC POLICE REVOLVER
FOR HOME AND POCKET

No. 881 Forehand & Wadsworth New Double Action, Self-Cocking Revolver, full nickel plated, rubber stock, rifled barrel, safe and reliable, accurate, rebounding locks, parts are interchangeable, 32 caliber, 2½ inch octagon barrel, weight 12 ounces. Our price.....$1.45
No. 882 38 caliber, 2½ inch octagon barrel, 5 shot, weight about 15 oz. Our price.....$1.45
Postage, extra, 17c.

Our $1.55 Revolver.

No. 883 Forehand & Wadsworth Safety hammer, double action Revolver, full nickel plated, rubber stock, rifled barrel, rebounding lock, safe, reliable and accurate, 32 caliber, 2½ inch octagon barrel, 6 shot, weight 12 ounces.
Our price.....$1.55
No. 884 38 caliber, 2½ inch octagon barrel, 5 shot, weight 15 oz. Our price.....$1.55
Postage, extra, 17c.

Harrington & Richardson Automatic Revolvers.

Our $2.85 Automatic.

No. 885. This revolver would retail in any first-class gun store at from $5 to $6. It is the celebrated Harrington & Richardson improved automatic, self extracting, double action, self-cocking revolver, modeled on the Smith & Wesson pattern, beautifully nickel plated, rubber stock, as accurate and durable as any revolver on the market and equal to the Smith & Wesson in shooting. Weight 18¾ oz., 3¼ inch barrel, 6 shot, 32 caliber, center fire.
Our price.....$2.85
No. 886. 5 shot, 38 caliber, central fire.
Our price.....$2.85
Postage, extra, 22c.

Our $2.70 Revolver.

No. 887. The Celebrated Forehand & Wadsworth Automatic Revolver for $2.70, a revolver that retails at from $5.00 to $6.00. The very latest improved model, automatic shell extractor, rebounding locks, double action, self-cocking, simple and accurate, interchangeable parts made from drop steel forgings. The frame is cast steel, no malleable iron about it, nickel plated throughout, fancy rubber stock, every revolver is fully warranted, length of barrels 3¼ inches, weight 17 oz., entire length 7⅝ inches. The fact that we sold over 10,000 of these revolvers during the last year is evidence of the general satisfaction they give. 32 caliber, Smith & Wesson center fire cartridges, 6 shot.
Our price.....$2.70
No. 888. 38 caliber, Smith & Wesson center fire cartridges, 6 shot. Our price.....$2.70
No. 889. Either 32 or 38 caliber with 5 inch barrel. Our price.....$3.45
We can furnish these revolvers in blued finish when so desired at 50c. extra.
Postage, 25c extra; 5 inch barrels, 35c extra.

NOTICE: Owing to the heavy advance at the factory, in the price of Revolvers, our present prices apply to STOCK ON HAND, and are subject to change without notice. Take advantage of our low prices and order at once.

No. 8314. Center fire, 38 caliber, ext... powder, 148 grains lead, for Ballard... box, 52c; per 100, $1.67; weight 2¼ lbs...

38 W.C.F.

8315

Per box, 69c; per 100, $1.38; weight 2¾...

No. 8316. Cartridges, center fire, 34 caliber for Colt's Lightning Repeating Rifle, 40 grains powder, 180 grains lead.
Per box of 50, 70c; per 100, $1.37; w... per box.

NEW LIGHTNING MAGAZINE

8316

COLTS.D.A.

8317

No. 8318. Cartridges, Colt's revolver, ... fire (short DA), 50 in a box. Per ... $1.15; weight 1½ lbs. per box.

No. 8319. Cartridges, 44 caliber Smith & Wesson, center fire, No. 3 Russian, 50 in a box. Per box, 80c; per 100, $1.42; weight 2¼ lbs.

44S&W.R

8319

BALLARD & MAR

100.....
No. 8329. Cartridges, for Ballard, Mar... 32-40 caliber, 13 grains of powder, ... 48c.; per 100.....

BALLARD & MAR

weight, 1¼ lbs., 60c.; per 100 $2.72.
No. 8331. Cartridges, for Ballard, Mar... short range. 20 grains of powder. ... Per box of 20, 60c.; per 100.....

WINCHESTE
MODEL 1886
40-60 COL
NEW LIGHTNING MAG
WINCHEST
MODEL 188
40-60 MARLI

No. 8336½. Cartridges for Wincheste... Per box..... Per 100.....
No. 8337. Cartridges, 40-70-330, straig... of 20, 79c.; trade price per 100.....

DID YOU EVER HEAR OF ...

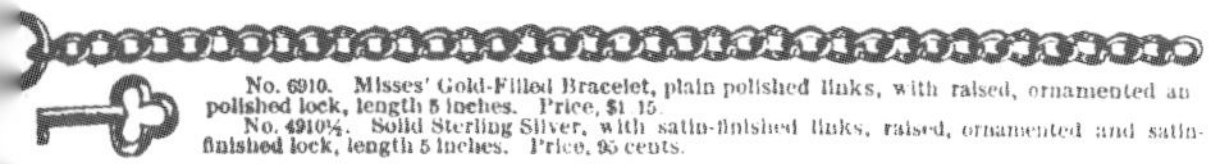

In Gold-Filled and Silver Bracelets we handle nothing but the finest quality, and our line embraces all of the desirable patterns on the market. Chain Bracelets are now the most stylish. They are all full length and are adjustable. Our Gold-Filled Bracelets are all warranted to wear and retain their color for twenty years.

No. 6910. Misses' Gold-Filled Bracelet, plain polished links, with raised, ornamented and polished lock, length 5 inches. Price, $1.15.
No. 4910½. Solid Sterling Silver, with satin-finished links, raised, ornamented and satin-finished lock, length 5 inches. Price, 95 cents.

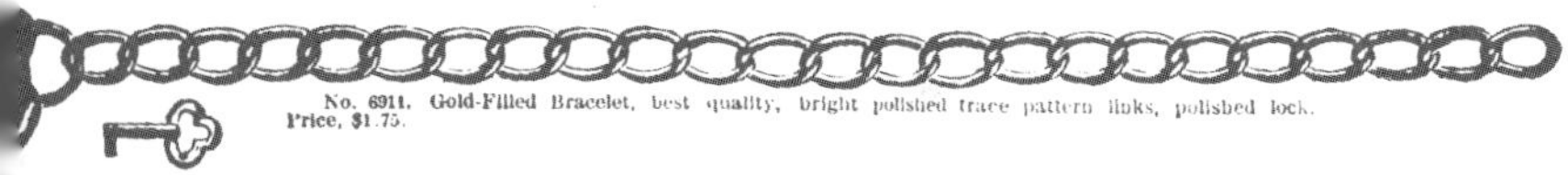

No. 6911. Gold-Filled Bracelet, best quality, bright polished trace pattern links, polished lock. Price, $1.75.

No. 6912. Gold-Filled Bracelet, best quality, fancy chased links, raised, ornamented and polished lock. Price, $2.00.

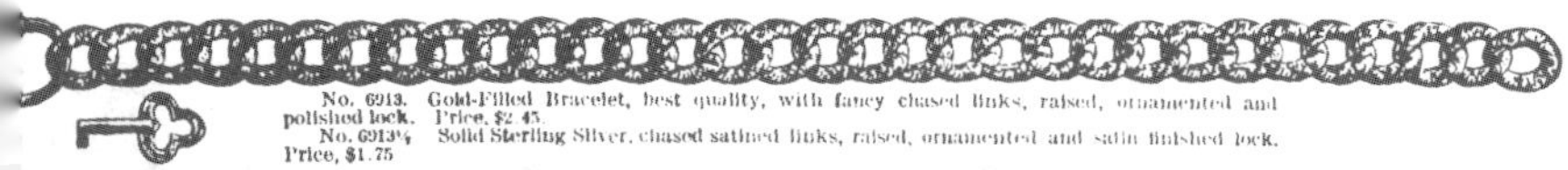

No. 6913. Gold-Filled Bracelet, best quality, with fancy chased links, raised, ornamented and polished lock. Price, $2.45.
No. 6913½ Solid Sterling Silver, chased satined links, raised, ornamented and satin finished lock. Price, $1.75

THE NEW ITHACA EJ

THE NEW ITHACA HAMMER GUN FOR $19.95.
This is the late improved model for 1896, manufactured by the Ithaca Gun Co., of Ithaca, New York.

THE C... EJ...
Grade A... tor; mad... Arms Co... N. Y. W... special t...